FREUD AND JUDAISM

FREUD AND JUDAISM

edited by
David Meghnagi

including
'Death and Us'
by Sigmund Freud

introduced and translated by
Mark Solms

Foreword by
Mortimer Ostow

London
KARNAC BOOKS

First published in 1993 by
H. Karnac (Books) Ltd.
58 Gloucester Road
London SW7 4QY

Copyright © 1993 by David Meghnagi

'Death and Us' by Sigmund Freud
translation and introduction copyright © 1993 by Mark Solms

All rights reserved. No part of this book may be reproduced,
in any form, by any process or technique,
without the prior written permission of the publisher.

British Library Cataloguing in Publication Data

Freud and Judaism
  I. Meghnagi, David
  150.1952

  ISBN 1-85575-002-3

Printed in Great Britain by BPCC Wheatons Ltd, Exeter

To my parents

CONTENTS

CONTRIBUTORS xi

FOREWORD
 Mortimer Ostow xv

PREFACE xxvii

1. **'Wir und der Tod'**
   A previously untranslated version of a paper
   by Sigmund Freud on the attitude towards death 1

   TRANSLATOR'S INTRODUCTION
    Mark Solms 3

   'Death and Us'
    Sigmund Freud 11

   EDITOR'S COMMENTS
    David Meghnagi 41

PART ONE
Judaism and psychoanalysis

2. A cultural event within Judaism
   David Meghnagi — 57

PART TWO
Historical aspects

3. Some thoughts on Freud's attitude during the Nazi period
   Janine Chasseguet-Smirgel — 73

PART THREE
Cultural aspects

4. The Jew as an ethical figure
   Silvia Vegetti Finzi — 95

5. Humour as a Jewish vocation and the work of Woody Allen
   Cesare Musatti — 103

PART FOUR
'Moses and Monotheism'

6. The logic of Freudian research
   Jorge Canestri — 117

PART FIVE
Applied psychoanalytic studies

7. Psychoanalysis between assimilation and proselytism
   Giorgio Sacerdoti — 133

8. Psychopathology of everyday antisemitism
    Antonio Alberto Semi   141

BIBLIOGRAPHY AND REFERENCES   153

INDEX   163

CONTRIBUTORS

DAVID MEGHNAGI, an author of essays on Freud and psychoanalytical clinical studies, is an associate member of the Italian Psychoanalytical Society. He lectures and researches at the University of Rome, where he co-ordinates the Research Unit for the Sociology of Judaism. He has been responsible for important research activities and psychoanalytic explorations relating to contemporary Jewish literature and to history, the psychology of humour, multilinguism, psychological experience in religion, and antisemitism. Among his publications are *Il Kibbutz: aspetti sociopsicologici* (Rome: Barulli, 1974), *La sinistra in Israele* (Milan: Feltrinelli, 1980), *Modelli freudiani della critica e teoria psicoanalitica* (Rome: Bulzoni, 1985), and *Il padre e la legge: Freud e l'ebraismo* (Venice: Marsilio, 1992).

JORGE CANESTRI, an author of essays on epistemology and psychoanalytical clinical studies, is a full member and training analyst of the Argentine Psychoanalytic Association and full member of the Italian Psychoanalytical Society. He has published (with J. Amati-Mehler and S. Argentieri) *La babele dell'inconscio. Lingua madre e lingua straniere nella dimensione psicoanalitica* (Milan: Raffaello Cortina, 1990).

JANINE CHASSEGUET-SMIRGEL was Chairperson of the Paris Psychoanalytical Society in 1975–76 and has been a member of the training committee of that society since 1964, the Vice Chairperson of the European Psychoanalytical Federation from 1970 to 1974, and the Freud Memorial Professor at University College, London, in 1982–83. She has published important studies in the field of theory and clinical research, which have been translated into several languages, and she has played a leading role in the International Psychoanalytical Association. Her works in English translation include *Creativity and Perversion, The Ego Ideal, Female Sexuality, Sexuality and the Mind,* and *Freud or Reich?*

SILVIA VEGETTI FINZI, a clinical psychologist with psychoanalytical training, lectures in Dynamic Psychology in the Department of Philosophy at Pavia University. She has published a history of psychoanalysis (*Storia della psicoanalisi: Autori opere teorie.* Milan: Mondadori, 1986).

CESARE MUSATTI, one of the pioneers of psychoanalytic and psychological research in Italy, was well known in politics and active in the defence of democratic values; for a long period, until his recent death, he was the Chairman of the Casa della Cultura in Milan. He published important contributions to the psychology of perception and to psychoanalysis. In 1938 he wrote the *Trattato di Psicoanalisi,* which was published after the war (Turin: Boringhieri, 1948). He planned and directed the Italian edition of the complete works of Sigmund Freud (*O.S.F.*; Turin: Boringhieri). He was Chairman of the Italian Psychoanalytical Society from 1951 to 1955 and Honorary President (together with another pioneer, Professor Emilio Servadio) from 1982 until his death.

GIORGIO SACERDOTI, an author of essays on psychoanalytic clinical studies and of *Irony through Psychoanalysis* (Karnac Books, 1992), is a full member and training analyst of the Italian Psychoanalytical Society, of which he has been Vice Chairman for more than three years, and a Founding Member of the Veneto Centre for Psychoanalysis. Until 1978 he worked as a psychiatrist in the Psychiatric Hospital Service in Venice, where he was Head of Department until 1958 and Director from 1968.

ANTONIO ALBERTO SEMI, a full member and training analyst of the Italian Psychoanalytical Society, is at present Chairman of the Veneto Centre for Psychoanalysis. He planned and edited the first volume of *Trattato di psicoanalisi. Teoria e tecnica*, (Turin: Boringhieri, 1948) as well as the second volume, *Trattato di Psicoanalisi. Clinica* (Milan: Raffaello Cortina, 1989–90).

MARK SOLMS is editor and translator of the forthcoming *Complete Neuroscientific Works of Sigmund Freud* and of the new Freud material to be included in the revised edition of his *Complete Psychological Works*. His previous publications include *A Moment of Transition: Two Neuroscientific Works by Sigmund Freud* (London: Karnac, 1990) and various articles in *The International Journal* and *International Review of Psycho-Analysis*. He is Honorary Lecturer at the London Hospital Medical College and a candidate of the British Psycho-Analytical Society.

FOREWORD

Curiosity, revelation, and applied psychoanalysis

Mortimer Ostow

The application of psychodynamic principles to individual and social problems produces results so interesting and promising that few psychoanalysts and psychoanalytically sophisticated scholars, proverbially curious, can resist such studies.

What are we curious to know? As adults what we most wish to know is the future—our individual future, our family's future, and our community's future. We're interested in the future with respect to health and sickness, birth and death, prosperity and decline, and success and failure. When we are in trouble, we long for a comforting vision. We hope to learn how a desperate situation can be repaired. Psychoanalysts recognize this hope as a wish for rebirth, which may be represented symbolically in fantasies and dreams by images suggesting literal birth. We also wish to learn how things work—our bodies, the natural world, the cosmos. We wonder and fantasize about those aspects of the lives of other people that are concealed from us—their sexuality, their intimacy, their happiness, and their grief. Society imposes an etiquette that dictates how much of our curiosity about these matters we may try to satisfy, how much must remain concealed, and how much we are permitted to reveal to others. To the extent that the objects of our curiosity are concealed from our direct view, we treat them as secrets.

Much knowledge possesses instrumental value. For animate organisms, curiosity helps to establish appropriate orientation in time and space, to locate potential prey and predators, to recognize potential mates and rivals, and so to establish social status, to distinguish between familiar and unfamiliar, between safety and hazard. Humans employ knowledge for these and for more complex functions, including operations dealing with food, shelter, social organization, health and comfort, and opportunity and danger, far as well as near. Moreover, for humans the acquisition of knowledge and its intellectual manipulation can provide pleasure. Information is vital for the pursuit of aggression and the defence against it.

A modern individual must find it difficult to imagine the effect upon the ancients of ignorance: not knowing how to explain natural phenomena, benign and dangerous; to protect themselves against illness and to alleviate it; and to anticipate attack from enemies, both close and remote. In the absence of useful data, the ancients—in fact, most individuals who lived before the scientific era and the availability of means of rapid transmission and diffusion of information—sought reassurance from pseudo-information, dreams as understood pre-scientifically, omens, portents, prophecies, and revelations. It seems reasonable to infer that need, giving rise to anxiety and fear, generates curiosity, perhaps instinctive in nature, which, even in the absence of true data, seeks 'information'. In general, the mood of the individual colours his perception of pseudo-data even more than it colours veridical data; the 'revelations' merely reinforce the existing mood of the subject.

Religion provides revelations that offer reassurance against fear. Examination of the contents of supernatural or magical revelations reveals that most exhibit the following components: the announcement of the revelation; a prophecy of destruction; and, in many instances, a prophecy of rebirth. We find such structures in the various kinds of scriptures, historical, legal, and prophetic. Exegesis is the process by which one attempts to extract meaning and guidance from a text beyond its plain meaning. The Mishnah and the Talmud, the post-scriptural instruments whereby biblical Judaism was transformed into rabbinical Judaism, base their arguments upon biblical prooftexts, thereby invoking the authority of biblical scripture to ensure the validity of rabbinical opinion. The writings of the early Church Fathers served a similar function in the Christian religion. These exegetical texts then became endowed with religious authority. During the Middle Ages, especially among the Jews, these texts were themselves subjected to exegetical examination and so became still another source of religious doctrine. In the absence of data, a hypercathected religious curiosity constructed mountains of speculation.

The religious revelation *par excellence* is the apocalypse. The word itself means revelation, and it almost always prophesies a cataclysmic destruction followed by a rebirth. The classical apocalypse is the Book of Revelation of the Christian bible. Religious and other social institutions sponsor myths of origin and myths of destiny.

Modern man looks to science to provide him with answers to his ultimate anxieties and uncertainties: the cosmos, the earth, external reality, the nature of life, our relations with other humans, how to prevent and treat illness. Mathematics codifies logical relations and permits us to manipulate them.

The media give us assurance that we know what is going on about us, both nearby and afar. Certainly the sciences and the news media offer us immeasurably greater reassurance against the danger of the unknown than had been available before the nineteenth century. Yet although the domain of the unknown has been slightly circumscribed and we are spared certain anxieties, we continue to project our inner anxieties upon the outside world. Given the amount of ignorance of the future that still prevails, external reality can easily be considered dangerous.

Accordingly, we still yearn for reassurances that neither science nor news can offer us. Some of us press science harder, hoping that as it develops, the domain of ignorance can be confined even further. However, the complete elimination of ignorance-based anxiety would require a degree of knowledge of external and internal processes that now seems unachievable. We approach complete knowledge asymptotically. We can eat from the tree of knowledge, but we cannot incorporate it completely. The more of science we know, the more we must acknowledge that it will never disclose to us a universe that is warm, hospitable, and loving. If we are to follow Freud in living by a 'scientific *Weltanschauung*', we shall have to do with accommodating ourselves to an inhospitable universe and an unkind reality.

Some moderns attribute the same power to revelations and magic that our ancestors did. Superstitions prevail broadly in our society. We extend all pseudo-sciences and create new ones: astrology, palm-reading, channelling, 'psychic' readings. Medical quackery falls into this category, as does attributing imaginary powers to authentic medical remedies—for example, attributing to vitamins or minerals curative powers that they have not been shown to possess.

While the tendency to seek magical solutions and secret knowledge and remedies cannot be considered pathognomonic of illness because it is so widespread, nevertheless we find it commonly associated with mental illness. We all know of certain patients who cannot tolerate reality and reject it in favour of beliefs based upon irrational procedures. One patient who was discontent with her lot in life regularly consulted a 'psychic' to learn the future, about which she was always reassured. Another patient, who had lost her mother at seven and remembered nothing about either that event or her experience of it, tried repeatedly to avoid facing reality by seeking the comforting forecasts of astrologers. She remembered no dreams and reported almost no inner life. She thought in terms of action, not ideas. She complemented her defensive ignorance with pseudo-information. The paranoiac who attributes significance to irrelevant signals, who credits delusions of reference, is seeking guidance by means of his pathologic curiosity. If the message he obtains is a threatening one, we must infer that his illness denies him the gratification that he seeks and threatens destruction.

Psychoanalysis is a scientific discipline that promises to disclose a different type of secret—the secrets that we each keep from ourselves. Until Freud, this type of secret was unsuspected. Nevertheless these secrets do answer some of our most archaic questions: they explain to us how we come to behave as we do, and they explain how others behave. Psychoanalysts contend that behaviour is not random or chaotic—even, or especially, when it is not rational. Psychoanalytic scrutiny does not permit us to predict the future, but it does point out some regularities in our own behaviour and in the behaviour of others who influence our lives. In addition, to the extent that we can apply psychodynamic principles to group behaviour, we might be able to anticipate possible courses of group action. In fact, the psychoanalytic method permits us to deal with the phenomenon of curiosity itself.

We can learn about the unconscious roots of curiosity from clinical material. In an essay based upon a splendid case history, Nunberg (1961) discusses the curiosity of children. It is directed, he says, towards three questions: the difference between the sexes; the nature of parental intercourse; and where babies come from. Nunberg's patient was frequently obsessed with questions to which he had to have ambiguous answers. The first recalled 'attack' of questioning began at the age of sixteen, when he asked himself 'when, precisely, the period of the Renaissance began and when it ended' (p. 170f.). The patient's associations led him to his first awareness of his sister's menstruation. Nunberg also points out that renaissance means rebirth, so that the question deals with birth. At another point the patient displayed an interest in origins in general: 'how the child is started; how it is born', as he put it. In this essay, Nunberg restricts himself to curiosity as a manifestation of childhood erotism. However, the question of rebirth and origins in general suggests other implications.

That Nunberg's analysis applies to social forces as well as to individual striving is demonstrated by the following quotation from the Talmud:

> One may not teach the subject of forbidden sexual relations in the presence of three people, nor the subject of the creation of the world even in the presence of two, nor the story (of the divine revelation by means) of the chariot (described in Ezekiel, Chapter 1). [*Babylonian Talmud*, Hagigah, 11b]

Here, too, we find Nunberg's triad: sexual intercourse, birth or origins, and the appearance of the parents' bodies, especially with regard to sexual characteristics. (Some of the symbolism specified in the first chapter of Ezekiel points directly to the genitals—cf. v. 27.)

A Jewish woman in her forties reported this dream, which, because of its relevance to my interests, I have quoted elsewhere (Ostow, 1986):

> There was wilderness and rubble. We had walked for miles to get there. I walked with a band of followers. I was there with a man with robes and a staff. The local people came to me. I asked about a structure like an old observation tower. It was cylindrical with a dome, high, at the edge of the town. An old priest, probably Christian. He believed that he was watching for the Messiah or Armageddon. Can I go up to ask him questions? Yes, but they kill people. I went upstairs inside the building. The man in robes met me. He had a dark beard. I had a manuscript that indicated that some old man would come and ask questions. I asked the questions, something about the staff. I can't remember the answers. He was not angry. He took me to a large window—an incredible view—you could see far off into the hills with the tower of stone. I was impressed that he had befriended me enough to show me this view.

First let us take note of the expressions of curiosity: I asked about a structure like an old observation tower; he was watching for the Messiah; can I ask him questions; I had a manuscript that indicated that some old man would come and ask questions; I asked the questions; I can't remember the answers; you could see far off into the hills with the tower of stone; he had befriended me enough to show me this view. That this was a phallic display was indicated by the manifest content: a man with robes and a staff; a structure like an old observation tower, which was cylindrical with a dome; he had a dark beard; questions, something about the staff; you could see . . . the tower of stone. That impression is reinforced by the patient's clear childhood memory of her father exhibiting his penis to her, both deliberately while urinating and presumably inadvertently when he appeared before her in pyjamas, the fly of which gaped.

However, the manifest dream suggests something in addition to a personal voyeuristic experience with her father. The 'wilderness and rubble' suggest a prevailing depressive effect. The 'band of followers', the Christian priest, the Messiah, Armageddon, the manuscript, all suggest a group-religious context—in fact, an apocalyptic context. This woman is looking for salvation from her depressive state of mind by searching for answers, a Messiah, and a manuscript. The curiosity serves two functions: it looks for the intimate voyeuristic gratification, and it also looks for personal salvation in a revelation. The man in robes, with the staff and beard, 'probably a Christian priest', represents the analyst, who—in the dream and in reality—is asked for two kinds of revelation: the genital exposure in which her father had indulged, and some saving or comforting words with respect to depression. We see in the dream that this curious patient hoped for personal sexual gratification and salvation by religious revelation from her depressive state, and she hoped to have these specifically from her analyst.

From Nunberg's material and its Talmudic antecedent, and this illustrative dream, we infer that curiosity subserves not only the gratification of early erotic needs, but also adult hope for rebirth, for rescue from serious distress. The patient may seek both of these gratifications in the analytic experience.

The wish to see, to hear, to experience, to know, results, I believe, in a wish to identify with the object of that desire. The story of the eating of the prohibited fruit in the Garden of Eden tells us that the acquisition of knowledge makes one like a divine being (Genesis III: 5, 22). Arlow (1951) pointed out the fact that the biblical prophets were consecrated by hallucinated, visual, and auditory immediate experience of God, and following this experience they felt identified with God—or at least felt that they could speak in His name and with His authority. [Arlow quotes an earlier paper by Otto Fenichel (1937), which refers to the aggressive wish to become like God through an act of scoptophilic introjection.] The gratification of curiosity then creates the possibility of identification, and the wish to see, hear, and learn may itself be motivated by the wish to identify with the parental saviour. Moreover, the erotic wish, the hope for salvation, and the eagerness to identify may all seek gratification within the same experience. We infer that curiosity, the desire to know, to understand, has an instinctual basis, the desire for erotic knowledge, the need to regenerate and to identify with the parental saviour. The instrumental value of knowledge directs our interest to those sources of information that are most useful and most revealing. The instinct contributes the passion that drives the quest for information. From the illusions that our curiosity spawns, we create individual myths, in order to provide a sense of order in our lives and dispel anxiety-provoking chaos. The groups to which we belong establish group myths that serve a similar function and invoke the credence of all of its members.

This book asks what Sigmund Freud and psychoanalysis can tell us about the origin, the life, and the destiny of Jews and the Jewish community. Presumably this for Jews is not just an academic exercise, nor is it pursued simply out of intellectual curiosity, as, for example, a work on psychoanalysis and art might be. While it is not without great intellectual interest, the answers relate to such practical issues as: how Jews think of themselves and behave in their relations with each other and with non-Jews; how they deal with antisemitism; how they think about their religion, history, and destiny; and what they transmit of Judaism to their children. One should not be surprised that psychoanalytically sophisticated individuals who are concerned with human problems will eagerly apply the methods and insights of psychoanalysis to them. And that would certainly apply to the concerns of Jews with the destiny of the Jewish people.

However, what we have here is not merely a set of comforting essays. Although that is what we consciously or unconsciously hope for, the authors in each case attempt to overcome our craving for illusion and myth, to sublimate the unconscious motivations of curiosity that we have discussed, and to come to grips with the realities, unpleasant as well as pleasant. As Freud repeatedly reminded us, true salvation can be found only in reality.

The principal subjects of the essays in this book are Freud and Moses—their and our views of Jewish origins and Jewish destiny. The quotation from Hagigah continues:

> As for him who concerns himself with the following four things, it would be better for him if he had never come into the world: what is above, what is below, what came before, and what comes after.

Applied psychoanalysis addresses itself to just those issues that Hagigah prohibits. These were prohibited because in the absence of information people constructed fantasies and myths expressing their wishes and the fears that the wishes generated—fantasies that were often self-defeating and socially disruptive, and myths that subverted the prescribed myths of the religion. Freud was impatient with the foundation myth of Judaism—that Moses, a heroic leader, introduced the Jews to their religion. Having become familiar with particular motifs in the psychology of individuals, Freud now ventured to propose that there was a patricide in the pre-history of Judaism that repeated an archaic patricide of the primordial father. The repeated patricide left a residue of guilt, alleviated for the Christian by the expiatory power of the crucifixion of Jesus but still influencing the unpenitent Jews. He was replacing a religious myth by a psychoanalytic guess—perhaps another myth. We all, individuals and groups, require myths to satisfy our 'need for causality', to create an illusory order and dispel the mental chaos of ignorance.

These essays, in which psychoanalysis is seen as scientific—that is, realistic rather than magical—illuminate the way in which Jews might survive in the modern world, both in theory and in practice. This is the rational counterpart to messianic illusions, the legend of the golem, and even the mythical antecedents of Freud's metaphor, the 'witch of metapsychology'. Although psychoanalysis may be regarded unconsciously as a source of salvation, a secret revelation, it is used here as a means of ascertaining realistic and practical answers to real questions.

The first essay in the book, Freud's B'nai B'rith speech on the meaning of death, exemplifies the attitude of the applied psychoanalyst. We approach an essay with the title, 'Death and Us', eagerly hoping, at least unconsciously, that the discoverer of psychoanalysis has something to tell us about death that will make it easier for us to tolerate, less terrible, less inevitable. But the hoped-for comforting revelation does not appear. Freud tells us that if we wish really to live, we must be prepared to meet death.

David Meghnagi comments on Freud's essay, seeing it as a point of departure for Freud's subsequent excursions into the nature of Judaism—not simply the Jewish religion, but the entire Jewish enterprise. Contemplating the horrors of World War I and of continuing and increasing antisemitism, Freud, he says, is examining the sources of 'civilized' behaviour and searching for an appropriate Jewish response. Freud is applying his psychoanalytic understanding to ascertaining what, if anything, can be saved, and what is the most useful attitude for Jews, for all minorities, and for civilized people.

In the following essay, Meghnagi expresses the view that psychoanalysis was devised as a response to the Jewish situation prevailing in Europe at that time. It explores the *mystery* of Jewish destiny and tries to find *answers*. He comments on other proposed *solutions*—Zionism, socialism, secularism, assimilation, conversion, all of which were advanced at different periods. Meghnagi relates Freud's work in psychoanalysis to the other scientific and scholarly endeavours of the time, undertaken by his Jewish contemporaries, with the intention of finding 'a grand new idea of humanity that was valid for everyone'.

Chasseguet-Smirgel examines Freud's attitudes during the 1930s, in order to defend him against the accusations of those who have used his public statements to disparage him. Chasseguet-Smirgel is a splendid psychoanalyst and writes with a strong sense of justice, and here she performs a service for all of us in maintaining the integrity of the image of the founder of psychoanalysis against his scoptophilic detractors.

In his essay on Jewish humour, Musatti uses the psychoanalytic approach to humour to discern how Jewish humour reflects the Jew's view of himself in a gentile world.

Canestri, in his essay on Freud's Moses, considers Freud's motivation to speculate—indeed, his compulsion—and he suggests that his search for solutions for the group was impelled by the need to quiet his own turmoil. Canestri is impressed by the strength of the curiosity that overrides Freud's usual clinical caution and political tact. In drawing our attention to Freud's adherence to the necessity of distinguishing between the pleasure principle and the reality principle, he reminds us of the distinction between illusory revelation and realistic analysis—a distinction that marked the beginning of the Enlightenment.

In 'Zakhor', Yosef Haim Yerushalmi's (1982) magisterial essay on Jewish historiography, he argues that,

> Today Jewry lives a bifurcated life. As a result of the emancipation in the Diaspora and national sovereignty in Israel Jews have fully re-entered the mainstream of history, and yet their perception of how they got there and where they are is most often more mythical than real. Myth and memory condition action. There are myths that are life sustaining and deserve to be reinterpreted for our age. There are some that lead astray and must be redefined. Others are dangerous and must be exposed. [pp. 99–100]

Meghnagi and his associates here deploy the methods of applied psychoanalysis for the purpose of addressing specifically this assignment.

PREFACE

After first having been denied, the Jewish element in the works of Freud has been studied from many different points of view. In Italy the debate has recently been enriched by the translation of *Freud: A Life for Our Time* (1988), *A Godless Jew* (1987), and *Freud, Jews and other Germans* (1979) by Peter Gay, and by the seminar that sparked off the present volume.[1]

In this collection of essays, which are wide-ranging in terms of approach and style, there can be found studies that are representative of the tendencies in research during the last few years: from the biographical and psychological approach explaining this connection through the existence of a 'particular Jewish tendency' or 'outlook' deriving from the specific social and existential condition of the Jew in modern society (Musatti), to the approach establishing a parallel between the history of thought and of the psychoanalytic institution on the one hand and the history of contemporary Judaism in the face of the phenomenon of assimilation on the other (Sacerdoti); from the reconstruction of the historical context in which Freud found himself working (Chasseguet-Smirgel), to the identification of anti-Jewish drives within clinical practice itself (Semi).

In the two essays on Moses (Canestri and Finzi) links are sought between Freud's scientific production and his personal meditation on Judaism, and between his own personal myths and the connection of those with the plan to evolve a positive theory of Judaism in reply to the outbreak of antisemitic racism.

This is an attempt to focus on a vast and complex problem—one that has not yet been systematically approached. The problem of inferences cannot be said to be exhausted yet. Owing to the richness and complexity of the questions arising from it, the issue can be reconsidered from a different point of view which aims at understanding the links and connections deriving from what historians see as the heredity of a long period. I refer, to quote only the most authoritative example, to the results of Scholem's monumental research on the part played by the heresies that shook Judaism in the seventeenth century in the affirmation of a *'forma mentis'* predisposed to accept lay and liberal enlightened ideology, among the generation born a century later. This chapter in history goes beyond the clarifying of aspects that are far removed from Jewish history and involves the very inner dialectics of the birth of the modern world: one might think of Baruch Spinoza and how his philosophical reflection is related to the upsetting of Jewish life following the drama of the forced conversions and the expulsions of 1492. In this light, 'Freud and Judaism' becomes a problem that paradoxically goes beyond the person of the founder of psychoanalysis and his direct relationship with Jewish tradition. Basically, Freud's Moses project revolves around issues of this kind—although the fact that phylogenetic evasions and Lamarckian hypotheses condemn the author right from the start is another question . . .

It is to the enigma of the man Moses that all Freudian reflection on Judaism leads. But it is also the point of convergence for the unresolved questions on Freud's writings relating to the very meaning of analysis and its limits in the face of the profound dynamism of human civilization. It may seem paradoxical, but it is precisely because of 'an entirely Jewish question' that such issues, which have always been present in Freud (one might think of his writings on civilization), have dramatically come to the fore again, at the same time bringing to light the unresolved problem of the relationship between historical and mythical–symbolic dimensions. From 'Oedipus' to 'Moses', from Greek tragedy to the rendering explicit of the drama that has 'always' been at the heart of Jewish consciousness—to paraphrase Kafka—psychoanalysis is a 'Jewish story'.

NOTE

1. I would like to remember Professor Cesare Musatti, past honorary president of the Italian Psychoanalytical Society, who, as a chairman of the Case della Cultura, gave me his support for the planning and the preparation of the scientific part of the programme. The seminar that gave rise to this book was sponsored by the Casa della Cultura in Milan and held on 27–28 May 1989. The seminar was held as a joint venture with the Sigmund Freud Center at the Hebrew University of Jerusalem, to celebrate the fiftieth anniversary of the late Sigmund Freud. I would like to thank Sergio Scalpelli, the director of the Casa della Cultura, and his staff for their help; the members of the honorary committee of the seminar: Sidney Blatt, Francesco Corrao, Giovanni Hautmann, Joseph Sandler, and Janine Chasseguet-Smirgel; and all the contributors: Jorge Canestri, Elvio Fachinelli, Silvia Vegetti Finzi, Enzo Funari, Gavriel Levi, Meriem Meghnagi, Enzo Morpurgo, Giorgio Sacerdoti, and Antonio Alberto Semi.

FREUD AND JUDAISM

CHAPTER ONE

'*WIR UND DER TOD*'
A previously untranslated version
of a paper by Sigmund Freud
on the attitude towards death

TRANSLATOR'S INTRODUCTION

Mark Solms

On 16 February 1915 Freud presented the lecture translated below—*Wir und der Tod* ['Death and Us']—to the Vienna lodge of the International Order of the B'nai B'rith (the Sons of the Covenant).[1]

Freud had been a member of the B'nai B'rith since 29 September 1897 and had addressed it on numerous previous occasions. Included among the earlier lectures were the following titles: 'The Interpretation of Dreams' (presented in December, 1897); 'The Psychology of Forgetting' (February, 1899); 'The Mental Life of the Child' (February, 1900); 'Chance and Superstition' (February, 1901); 'On Dreams' (April, 1902); 'The Physiology of the Unconscious' (1905); 'Psychology in the Service of

---

Generous assistance with various aspects of this work from Silke Heiß, Karen Kaplan-Solms, Ingeborg Meyer-Palmedo, Mortimer Ostow, Cesare Sacerdoti, and Astra Temko is gratefully acknowledged. Also, I am indebted to David Meghnagi for first drawing my attention to this lecture and for inviting me to translate it.

[1] Strachey (1957) gave the date of this address as April, 1915.

the Administration of Justice' (March, 1907); 'The Problem of Hamlet' (1911); and 'What Is Psycho-Analysis' (November, 1913).[2] The reader will readily deduce from these titles—and from the dates of their presentation—that the B'nai B'rith lectures served as models for some celebrated publications by Freud.

The special interest attached to 'Death and Us' is that it is the only lecture in this series that was ever published[3]—and the only one, therefore, that survives today. It has long been recognized that this lecture was the basis for the second part of Freud's 'Thoughts for the Times on War and Death' (1911b)— that is, for his essay entitled 'Our Attitude Towards Death' (*'Unser Verhältnis zum Tode'*; see Jones, 1953–57, Vol. 2; Strachey, 1957). However, the fact that this lecture was *published* has only recently been rediscovered (D. B. Klein, 1981).[4] The aim of the present chapter, therefore, is to make this unique document available to English-speaking scholars of psychoanalysis.

The singularity of the document resides in the fact that it is the only known text by Freud that exists in two distinct versions. It is true that rough drafts and notes for some well-known works by Freud have been published, as have transcripts of some unpublished manuscripts; and it is also true that Strachey's meticulous footnotes to the *Standard Edition* trace chronological revisions of those of his works that appeared in multiple editions; but there is no other single text that exists in two

---

[2] See D. B. Klein (1981) for a complete list of Freud's lectures to the B'nai B'rith, and for a reconstructed summary of their contents. See also Editor's Comment, pp. 41–52.

[3] The lecture was published, within weeks of its delivery, in the *Zweimonats-Bericht für die Mitglieder der österr. israel. Humanitätsvereine B'nai B'rith*, *18* (1): 41–51.

[4] The existence of the published lecture was not recognized, for example, in Richards's (1974) Freud Bibliography to the *Standard Edition*, *24*. It was, however, included in the much-revised and updated bibliography compiled by Meyer-Palmedo & Fichtner (1989), and it has since been reprinted in the popular German periodical, *Die Zeit* (Nitzschke, 1990), and in the Jewish section ('Itinerari ebraici'), edited by D. Meghnagi, of the European Review, *Lettera Internazionale*, *26* (6) (October–December, 1990), pp. 23–43.

deliberate versions, written more-or-less simultaneously, for two different audiences.

The first version of this lecture was composed for *oral* presentation, to a *lay*, almost exclusively *Jewish* audience—an audience for which Freud felt considerable personal affection.[5] In the second version the lecture was rewritten as an essay, expressly for *printed* publication, in a *specialist* journal, with a predominantly *psychoanalytical* readership.[6] Comparison of the two versions could, therefore, provide new insights into Freud's methods and style of working—as a writer and an orator—into the way in which he thought about the concepts and ideas discussed in this work, and, indeed, into some aspects of his public persona and his personality as a whole.

With these possibilities in mind, the present chapter is arranged as follows.

We are dealing with four texts:

a. the original German version of a lecture presented to the B'nai B'rith, first published in 1915 in the *Zweimonats-Bericht für die Mitglieder der österr. israel. Humanitätsvereine B'nai B'rith*;[7]

---

[5] See D. B. Klein (1981) for a comprehensive account and appraisal of Freud's relationship with the B'nai B'rith. See also Editor's Comments, pp. 41–52.

[6] In *Imago*, 4 (1): 1-21. It seems likely that Freud had not initially intended to publish the lecture in this format, but that he did so in response to pressure from the publisher, Heller, who had complained of a dearth of material for the journal. (See Jones, 1953–57, Vol. 2, who cites a letter from Freud to Abraham, dated March 4, 1915. See also Strachey, 1957, who suggests that the revisions were executed in March or April, 1915).

[7] There are a few minor (mainly typographical) variations between this edition of the lecture and the 1990 reprinting published in *Die Zeit* (cf. footnote 5). Interesting as these variations are—for they demonstrate the subtle influence that even a typesetter can have on the eventual published text—they are not specifically identified and discussed here. The main purpose of this chapter is, firstly, to make available in English translation the original (*1915*) version of the B'nai B'rith lecture and, secondly, to compare that lecture with the *1915* essay based upon it. This task alone produces an intricate and sometimes bewildering web of information, which would be unnecessarily complicated by further, extraneous detail.

b. an English translation of that lecture, published here for the first time;[8]

c. the original German version of an essay, based upon the B'nai B'rith lecture, first published in 1915 in *Imago*;[9]

d. the English translation by James Strachey of that essay, published in the *Standard Edition*.[10]

Text *b*, the first English translation of the 1915 lecture, occupies the *main body* of the present chapter. This translation is punctuated, at regular intervals, by *footnotes* that compare the equivalent passages in the revised, *essay* version (i.e. in text *d*). The differences between these two versions are indicated to the reader in the footnotes by means of **bold type**.

In a few isolated instances it was necessary to make minor modifications to Strachey's authoritative translation in order to convey subtle differences between the two German versions.[11] All modifications of this sort are clearly identified as such in the footnotes.

Thus—barring the exceptions just mentioned—the English translation of the B'nai B'rith lecture presented in the main body of the text below (i.e. text *b*) differs from Strachey's *Standard Edition* translation of the *Imago* essay (i.e. text *d*) in a manner that exactly parallels the differences that existed between the two original German versions—texts *a* and *c*.

---

[8] D. B. Klein (1981) translated a few isolated sentences from the lecture.

[9] As was the case for the lecture, numerous typographical and other variations exist between the first and subsequent German editions of the essay (cf. the *Sammlung kleiner Schriften zur Neurosenlehre*, 4; *Gesammelte Schriften*, *10*; *Internationaler Psychoanlytischer Verlag* edition of 1924; *Gesammelte Werke*, *10*; and *Studienausgabe*, *9*)—variations which are not explicitly referred to below.

[10] Two other English translations of this text have been published, the first by Brill & Kuttner (1918) and the second by Mayne (1925). Again, the differences between these and Strachey's translations, and indeed, the variations between the *Standard* and Pelican editions of Strachey's (1957) translation, are not commented upon here.

[11] Strachey was, of course, unaware that the B'nai B'rith lecture existed in published form and therefore could not take it into account when he translated the essay version.

TRANSLATOR'S INTRODUCTION 7

The reader will see that Freud subjected the B'nai B'rith lecture to a very thorough revision before he published it in the essay form. In most respects, however, these changes are barely perceptible at first reading. Apart from a few obvious deletions (consisting mainly of passages of exclusively Jewish interest) and equally few additions (essentially of scholarly references and the like), the two versions of this work appear at first to be identical. It is only on much closer examination that the pervasive but subtle shift in emphasis and style from the lecture to the essay becomes apparent. In fact, only a handful of sentences across the two versions are exactly alike.

The differences between the two texts can be broadly characterized as follows.

1. Firstly, as mentioned above, all passages of *exclusively Jewish interest* are expunged in the *Imago* version. The most obvious example of this type is to be found in the opening lines of the text, where Freud suggests that he might have amended the title of his lecture:

> Instead of: 'Death and *Us*', it could have read: 'Death and *Us Jews*', for it is precisely we Jews who reveal most frequently and in the most extreme ways the attitude towards death that I wish to deal with before you today.

Other examples of this type are to be found in footnotes 1, 5, 16, 29, and 41.

2. Also deleted from the *Imago* version are numerous jokes and anecdotes, some of which are of a specifically Jewish character (see footnotes 5 and 16), others not (footnotes 5, 18, 46, 53, 54). The omission of such material has the effect of decreasing the *immediacy and directness of contact* between the author and his audience. This diminution of immediacy and directness is effected in other ways as well. Thus, for example, Freud made frequent use of rhetorical questions (cf. footnotes 2, 5, 20, 24, 25) and of first- and second-person references (footnotes 5, 6, 15, 17, 21, 23, 30, 38, 45, 46, 49, 51–55, 58, 61) in the lecture, all of which are deleted in the *Imago* version.

3. The tone of the lecture is also *more tentative and sympathetic* than that of the essay. Freud seems to have been extraordinarily sensitive to the uncomfortable feelings that his topic

might have evoked in his audience (see footnotes 6 and 24). In the opening paragraph of the text, for example, Freud actually apologizes for the very subject-matter of his lecture:

> Please do not suppose that I gave my lecture such an eerie title in order to upset you. I know that there are many people who wish to have nothing to do with death—perhaps, therefore, amongst yourselves too—and I wanted to avoid luring these Brethren into a lecture that would distress them.

Similarly, at one point, when discussing the war, Freud identifies himself with the patriotic feelings of his German-speaking audience (see footnote 45). Freud also took greater care in the lecture to orientate his audience to the unfolding argument, by means of frequent examples, reminders of points already established, and references to forthcoming conclusions (see footnotes 1, 6, 24, 46, 54, 56).

4. Other changes of a similar kind relate to the fact (already mentioned above) that the essay version was directed to *a specialist psychoanalytical readership*, whilst the original B'nai B'rith lecture was addressed primarily to a *lay* audience (see footnotes 5, 6, 19, 23, 28, 32, 46, 49, 55). Here Freud's choice of everyday language to represent technical terms is of particular interest. In the lecture version, for example, he describes psychoanalysis as being 'a sort of *under-water psychology*'. Similarly, the term 'unconscious impulses' in the *Imago* version corresponds to 'unspoken thoughts' in the lecture version, and the phrase 'cravings of the lust to kill' in the lecture version corresponds to 'hostile impulse' in the essay. Other changes of a comparable sort consist in expansions and improvements of the arguments originally presented in the lecture, and in additions of scholarly material such as references and annotations (see footnotes 6, 8, 14, 20, 27, 28, 31, 32, 33, 36, 37, 42–46, 51, 52, 58, 59, 61).

5. Finally, the *grammar and style* of Freud's language in the *Imago* version is *more formal and correct* than it was in the lecture (see footnotes 8, 14, 15, 17, 18, 20, 22, 27, 28, 32, 35, 39, 45, 46, 48, 49, 52, and 60). This is due in part to the requirements of oral versus written presentation, but also to the fact that the two versions were addressed to different audi-

TRANSLATOR'S INTRODUCTION 9

ences. However, some of the changes in syntax and grammar are rather painstaking and might appear to the reader to serve little objective purpose, such as alterations in the punctuation, switching the order of words, substituting synonyms, and so on (see footnotes 9, 13, 17, 19, 20–22, 26, 30, 39, 48–50, 55, 60). Thus, for example, '**a** child or **a** friend' in the lecture version becomes 'child or **close** friend' in the essay; the phrase 'whom he **certainly** loved' becomes 'whom he **undoubtedly** loved' in the essay; and '**impuls**ive **or instinct**ive' becomes '**instinct**ive **and impuls**ive'.

The implications of these changes for our understanding of Freud's cognitive style, his method of writing, his Jewish identity, and so on, are not specifically discussed in this chapter.[12]

---

[12]See, however, Editor's Comments, pp. 41–52.

'DEATH AND US'

Sigmund Freud

Honourable Presidents and dear Brethren,—Please do not suppose that I gave my lecture such an eerie title in order to upset you. I know that there are many people who wish to have nothing to do with death—perhaps, therefore, amongst yourselves too—and I wanted to avoid luring these Brethren into a lecture that would distress them. I could also have amended the other part of my title. Instead of: 'Death and *Us*', it could have read: 'Death and *Us Jews*', for it is precisely we Jews who reveal most frequently and in the most extreme ways the attitude towards death that I wish to deal with before you today.

However, you can easily imagine what led me to choose precisely this theme. It is a result of the terrible war that is raging at the moment, depriving us all of our bearings in life. I have observed, I believe, that foremost amongst the factors that are effecting this confusion is the change that has taken place in our attitude towards death.[1]

---

[1] [These two introductory paragraphs are replaced by the following one in the *Imago* version:]
The second factor to which I attribute our present sense of estrangement in this once lovely and congenial world is the **distur-**

What, then, is our approach towards death? In my opinion, it is very remarkable. On the whole, we behave as though we would like to eliminate death from life; we would like, so to speak, to hush it up; we think of it as though—'it were death'![2] Naturally, this tendency cannot prevail undisturbed. Death occasionally makes itself noticeable to us after all. Then we are deeply shaken, and torn from our security as though by something extraordinary. We say 'Terrible!' when a daring aviator or mountain-climber has an accident, when a collapsed scaffolding buries three or four workers, when twenty [female] apprentices perish in a blaze at a factory, or indeed, when a ship carrying a few hundred passengers is lost. We are affected most when death has struck down one of our acquaintances; when it is a B['nai] B['rith] Brother we even hold a funerary meeting [*Trauersitzung*]. But no one could conclude from our behaviour that we recognize death as a necessity, that we are certain in our conviction that each one of us owes Nature his death.[3] On the contrary, we always find an explanation that reduces this necessity to chance. That one over there, who died, had an infectious pneumonia—of course it wasn't necessary; the other had been very ill for a long time already, he just didn't realize it; a third was, of course, very old and frail.[4] Indeed, when one of us—a Jew—dies, then we would have to conclude that a Jew never dies of natural causes at all. At the very least a doctor must have done him damage, otherwise he would still be alive today. Although it is conceded that one must eventually die, we tend to shift this 'eventually' into the unforeseeable future. When one asks a Jew how old he is, he likes to answer: Sixty (or thereabouts) to one-hundred-and-twenty!

---

bance that has taken place in **the** attitude **which we have hitherto adopted** towards death.

[The 'disillusionment of the war' was the first factor.]

[2] [An allusion to the German saying, '*Man denke an etwas wie an den Tod*' ('to think of something as though it were death')—i.e. to think something unlikely or incredible (cf. footnote 5 below).]

[3] [An allusion to Prince Hal's remark to Falstaff in *Henry IV*, Part I, 4, ii: 'Thou owest God a death' (cf. footnote 5 below).]

[4] Compare this with the admonition: '*On meurt à tout âge*' ['One dies at any age'].

'DEATH AND US' 13

The psycho-analytic school, which, as you know, I represent, has ventured on the claim that at bottom we—each one of us—do not believe in our own death. In any event, it is impossible for us to imagine. At every attempt to picture how things might be after our death, by whom we might be mourned etc., we may notice that we are still there as observers after all. Indeed, it is most difficult to instil in someone a sense of this inevitability. As soon as he is in a position to have the decisive experience [i.e. death], he becomes inaccessible to evidence of every kind![5]

To reckon upon someone else's death; only a hard-hearted or wicked person would think of such a thing. Kinder and more proper people—like all of us—struggle against such thoughts, especially if some advantage to ourselves in freedom, posi-

---

[5] [The above two paragraphs correspond to the following one in the *Imago* version:]

That attitude was far from straightforward. To anyone who listened to us we were of course prepared to maintain that death was the necessary outcome of life, that everyone owes Nature a death **and must expect to pay the debt—in short, that death was natural, undeniable and unavoidable. In reality, however, we were accustomed to behave as if it were otherwise. We showed an unmistakable tendency to put death on one side,** to eliminate it from life. **We tried** to hush it up; **indeed we even have a saying: 'to think of something** as though it were death'. **That is, as though it were our own death, of course.** It is indeed impossible to imagine **our own death; and whenever we** attempt to **do so we can perceive** that we are **in fact** still **present as spectators. Hence** the psycho-analytic school **could venture** on the **assertion** that at bottom **no one** believes in his own death, **or, to put the same thing in another way, that in the unconscious every one of us is convinced of his own immortality.**

[However, the remarks upon the tendency to reduce death from necessity to chance—when one is compelled to acknowledge death by its occurrence in reality—and the 'terrible' shock at multiple deaths in mass tragedies, are shifted to the next paragraph (footnote 6 below).

Incidentally, the age 'one-hundred-and-twenty' mentioned in the *Imago* text above probably refers to the fact that this is considered the optimal life-span in traditional Jewry. The number is based upon the account of Moses's death (aet. 120) at the end of the Book of Deuteronomy.]

tion or assets could result from the death of the other person.[6] Should the other person, perchance, die after all, then we admire him almost as if he were a hero who has accomplished an extraordinary task. If we were hostile towards him we reconcile ourselves with him; we abandon our criticism of him: '*De mortuis nil nisi bonum*';[7] we like to see fanciful praise inscribed upon his tombstone.[8] We are, however, completely helpless when death has taken someone who is dear to us—a parent or a

---

[6] [The last two sentences are modified and expanded as follows in the *Imago* version:]

When it comes to someone else's death, **the civilized man will carefully avoid speaking of such a possibility in the hearing of the person under sentence. Children alone disregard this restriction; they unashamedly threaten one another with the possibility of dying, and even go so far as to do the same thing to someone they love, as, for instance: 'Dear Mummy, when you're dead I'll do this or that.' The civilized adult can hardly even entertain the thought of another person's death without seeming to himself** hard-hearted or wicked; **unless, of course, as a doctor or lawyer or something of the kind, he has to deal with death professionally. Least of all will he allow himself to think of the other person's death** if some **gain** to **himself** in freedom, **property** or position **is bound up with it. This sensitiveness of ours does not, of course, prevent the occurrence of deaths; when one does happen, we are always deeply affected, and it is as though we were badly shaken in our expectations. Our habit is to lay stress on the fortuitous causation of death—accident, disease, infection, advanced age; in this way we betray an effort to reduce death from a necessity to a chance event. A number of simultaneous deaths strikes us as something extremely terrible.**

[7] ['Speak nothing but good of the dead.']

[8] [The last two sentences are modified and expanded as follows in the *Imago* version:]

Towards the actual person who has died we adopt a special attitude—something almost like **admiration for someone who has** accomplished **a very difficult** task. We **suspend** criticism of him, **overlook his possible misdeeds, declare that** '*de mortis nil nisi bonum*', **and think it justifiable to set out all that is most favourable to his memory in the funeral oration and** upon the tombstone. **Consideration for the dead, who, after all, no longer need it, is more important to us than the truth, and certainly, for most of us, than consideration for the living.**

'DEATH AND US' 15

partner in marriage, a brother or sister, a child or a friend.[9] Our hopes, our desires and our pleasures lie in the grave with him, we will not be consoled, we will not fill the lost one's place. We behave as if we were a kind of *Asra*, who *die when those they love die*.[10]

But this attitude of ours towards death has a powerful effect on our lives.[11] Life is impoverished, it loses in interest.[12] Our emotional ties, the unbearable intensity of our pain, make us

---

[9] [This sentence is expanded and modified into the following one (which begins a new paragraph) in the *Imago* version:]

The complement to this cultural and conventional attitude towards death is provided by our complete collapse when death has **struck down** someone who is **close** to us—a parent or a partner in marriage, a brother or sister, child or **dear** friend.

[Note that, in the original German, the word 'death' in the phrase 'when death has taken someone/struck down someone' reads '*der Tod*' in the 'B'nai B'rith version and '*das Sterben*' in the *Imago* version. The meaning is, however, identical, and the variation cannot be meaningfully reflected in the English translation. Also, the phrase 'a child or a friend/dear friend' reads '*ein Kind oder einen Freund*' in the first version and '*Kind oder teuren Freund*' in the *Imago* version. That is, apart from the insertion of '*teuren*' (dear), the words '*ein*' and '*einen*' (which are equivalent to the English indefinite article 'a' in this context, and therefore make no essential difference to the meaning) are deleted in the second version. This change is not reflected in Strachey's translation (*S.E.*, *14*, 290). Note also that Strachey translated '*uns nahestehenden Personen*' ('someone **who is close** to us') and '*oder teuren freund*' ('or **dear** friend') as 'someone **whom we love**' and 'or **close** friend' respectively (ibid.).

Regarding the translation of the term 'cultural', cf. footnote 45.]

[10] [An allusion to the tribe of Arabs in Heine's poem 'Der Asra', who 'die when they love'. In the original German, in both versions, the words 'Asra' and 'die when those they love die' are emphasized, but this is not reflected in Strachey's translation of the second version (*S.E.*, *14*, 290).]

[11] [This sentence, and the last two sentences in the previous paragraph, remain unchanged in the *Imago* version.]

[12] [This sentence is expanded as follows in the *Imago* version:]

Life is impoverished, it loses in interest, **when the highest stake in the game of living, life itself, may not be risked. It becomes as shallow and as empty as, let us say, an American flirtation, in which it is understood from the first that nothing is to happen, as**

16   SIGMUND FREUD

cowardly—inclined to avoid danger for ourselves and for those who belong to us. We dare not contemplate a great many undertakings that are in fact indispensable, such as attempts at artificial flight, voyages of discovery to distant countries or experiments with explosive substances.[13] We are paralysed by the thought of who is to take the son's place with his mother, the husband's with his wife, the father's with his children, if a disaster should occur, and yet all these undertakings are essential.[14] You know the motto of the Hanseatic League: '*Navigare necesse est, vivere non necesse*' ('It is necessary to sail the seas, it is not necessary to live').[15] In comparison, take what one of our very characteristic Jewish anecdotes expresses; the son falls off a ladder, remains lying there unconscious, and the mother runs to the Rabbi to seek help and

---

contrasted with a Continental love-affair in which both partners must constantly bear its serious consequences in mind.
[These expanded remarks appear, slightly modified, in the next paragraph of the B'nai B'rith version (cf. footnote 17 below).]

[13] [The last two sentences are slightly modified in the *Imago* version:] Our emotional ties, the unbearable intensity of our **grief**, makes us **disinclined to court** danger for ourselves and for those who belong to us. We dare not contemplate a great many undertakings which are **dangerous but** in fact indispensable such as attempts at artificial flight, **expeditions** to distant countries or experiments with explosive substances.
[Note that in the original German of the *Imago* version, the comma after 'indispensable' is deleted. This is not reflected in Strachey's translation (*S.E.*, *14*, 291).]

[14] [In the *Imago* version this sentence ends with the words 'if a disaster should occur', and the following sentence is added:]
Thus the tendency to exclude death from our calculations in life brings in its train many other renunciations and exclusions.

[15] [This sentence is slightly modified in the *Imago* version:]
Yet the motto of the *Hanseatic League* ran: 'Navigare necesse est, vivere non necesse!' ('It is necessary to sail the seas, it is not necessary to live').
[Note that in the original German of the *Imago* version, the term 'Hanseatic League' is emphasized and the motto (which ends in an exclamation mark) is not. These variations are not reflected in Strachey's translation (*S.E.*, *14*, 291).]

advice. 'Tell me', asks the Rabbi, 'how does a Jewish child come to be on a ladder [in the first place]?'[16]

I say that life loses in substance and interest when the highest stake, life itself, is excluded from its struggles. It becomes as hollow and shallow as an American flirtation, in which it is understood from the first that nothing is to happen, as contrasted with a Continental love-affair in which both partners must bear in mind its constantly lurking dangers.[17] We are obliged to make up for this impoverishment of life, and turn for this to the world of fiction, literature and the theatre. On the stage we find people who still know how to die—indeed, still can even kill others. Here we satisfy our wish that life itself should be preserved as a serious stake in life; and furthermore another wish is satisfied. That is, we would have nothing at all against death if it did not put an end to the life of which we have only one.[18] For it is really and truly too terrible that in life it should be just like it is in chess, where a single false move may force us to give up the game, but with the difference that we can start no second game, no return-match. In the realm of fiction we find the multiplicity of lives that we need. We die with the hero;

---

[16] [The last two sentences are deleted in the *Imago* version and this paragraph ends with the translation of the Hansean motto (as quoted in footnote 15 above; cf. *S.E.*, *14*, 291).]

[17] [This sentence is shifted, in the slightly modified form indicated below, to the previous paragraph in the *Imago* version (cf. footnote 12 above):]

It becomes as **shallow and empty** as, **let us say,** an American flirtation, in which it is understood from the first that nothing is to happen, as contrasted with a Continental love-affair in which both partners must **constantly bear its serious consequences** in mind.

[18] [This last sentence is deleted in the *Imago* version, and the previous three sentences (which begin the new paragraph) are modified as follows:]

It is an inevitable result of all this that we should seek in the world of fiction, **in** literature and **in** the theatre **compensation for what has been lost in life. There** we **still** find people who know how to die— **who,** indeed, **even manage to** kill **someone else. There alone too the condition can be fulfilled which makes it possible for us to reconcile ourselves with death: namely, that behind all the vicissitudes of life we should still be able to preserve a life intact.**

yet we survive him, and possibly die again, just as safely, with a second hero on another occasion.[19] Now what has war changed in this our attitude towards death? A great deal. Our death-conventions (as I would like to call them) can no longer be adhered to. Death is no longer overlooked; we are forced to believe in it. People are really dying; and no longer one by one, but many, often tens of thousands, in a single day. And death is no longer a chance event. To be sure, it still seems a matter of chance whether a bullet hits this man or that; but the accumulation of deaths soon puts an end to the impression of chance. Thus life, indeed, becomes interesting again; it has recovered its full content.[20]

---

[19] [The last two sentences are slightly modified in the *Imago* version:] For it is really **too sad** that in life it should **be as** it is in chess, where **one** false move may **compel** us to **resign** the game, but with the difference that we can start no second game, no return-match. In the realm of fiction we find the **plurality** of lives which we need. We die with the hero **with whom we have identified ourselves**; yet we survive him, and **are ready to die again** just as safely **with another hero**.

[Note that '*zwingen*' is here translated as 'compel' and '*nötigen*' as 'force'. Strachey, by contrast, translated '*zwingen*' as 'force' (*S.E., 14*, 291).]

[20] [This paragraph is slightly modified in the *Imago* version:]

It is evident that war **is bound to sweep away this conventional treatment of death.** Death **will** no longer **be denied**; we are forced to believe in it. People really **die**; and no longer one by one, but many, often tens of thousands, in a single day. And death is no longer a chance event. To be sure, it still seems a matter of chance whether a bullet hits this man or that, but **a second bullet may well hit the survivor; and** the accumulation of **deaths puts** an end to the impression of chance. Life **has**, indeed, **become** interesting again; it has recovered its full content.

[Three further modifications in the second version of the original German (grammatical and syntactical improvements) cannot be meaningfully reflected in English translation: the word 'day' is spelled '*Tag*' in the first version and '*Tage*' in the second; the word 'recovered' is equivalent to '*wiederbekommen*' in the first version and '*wieder bekommen*' (two words) in the second; and similarly, the phrase 'one by one' represents the word '*einzelne*' in the first version and '*einzeln*' in the second. Note that the semi-colon following the words 'this man or that' in the

Here a distinction should be made between two groups—those who are actually in the war and endanger their own lives, and those who have stayed at home and have only to wait for the loss of one of their beloved by wounds, infection and disease. It would be extremely interesting if we could study what mental changes are brought about in the combatants by the risking of their own lives. But I know nothing about this; I—like all of you—belong to the second group, to those who have stayed at home and can but tremble for their loved ones.[21] From my own case—and that of others in the same position—I have gained the impression that the numbness, the paralysis of capacity that has overcome us, is determined essentially by the one circumstance that we are unable to maintain our former attitude towards death, and have not yet found a new approach towards it. Now it may contribute to our new orientation if

---

first version is changed to a comma in the second version—which is not reflected in Strachey's translation (*S.E.*, *14*, 291).

Also note that the sentence, 'And death is no longer a chance event' corresponds to '**Er** [masculine] *ist auch kein Zufall mehr*' in the first version and '**Es** [neuter] *ist auch kein Zufall mehr*' in the second. Literally translated into English, the first version would amount to a personification of death.]

[21] [The last three sentences are modified as follows in the *Imago* version:]

Here a distinction should be made between two groups—those who **themselves risk their lives in battle**, and those who have stayed at home and have only to wait for the loss of one of **their dear ones** by wounds, **disease or infection**. It would be **most** interesting, **no doubt, to** study **the** changes **in the psychology of** the combatants, but I know **too little** about it. **We must restrict ourselves to** the second group, to **which we ourselves belong**.

[Also, in the original German, the phrase '*von den anderen trennen*' in the B'nai B'rith version is changed to the almost-identical phrase '*trennen von den anderen*' (perhaps more suited to written discourse) in the *Imago* version. Since this phrase disappears in the English translation (i.e. in the first sentence of Strachey's translation quoted above) the change is not reflected here. Further, the English 'at home' is given as '*zuhause*' in the first version and '*zu Hause*' (two words) in the second—another change which cannot be reflected in the translation (cf. footnote 20 above).]

together we inquire into two other relations to death—one of which we may ascribe to primaeval, prehistoric men, and one which still exists in every one of us, but which, invisible to consciousness, conceals itself in the deeper strata of mental life.[22]

Thus far, dear Brethren, I have told you nothing that you could not have known and felt just as well as I. Now I am in a position to tell you some things that you might not know, and some other things that you certainly shall not believe. I must put up with that.[23]

So what was the relationship of primaeval man towards death? He took up a very remarkable attitude in regard to death: it was far from consistent; it was indeed most contradictory. But we shall soon comprehend the reason for this contradiction.[24]

---

[22] [The last two sentences are slightly modified in the *Imago* version:] I **have already said that in my opinion** the **bewilderment and** the paralysis of capacity, **from which we suffer, are essentially** determined **among other things** by **the** circumstance that we are unable to maintain our former attitude towards death, and have not yet found a new **one**. It may **assist us to do this** if we **direct our psychological inquiry towards** two other relations to death—**the** one which we may ascribe to primaeval, prehistoric men, and **the** one which still exists in every one of us, but which, **invisible to consciousness,** conceals itself in the deeper strata of mental life.

[Note that the words 'to maintain' correspond to '*aufrechterhalten*' in the first version and '*aufrecht halten*' (two words) in the second. This insignificant change, again, cannot be meaningfully reflected in English translation. Also, there is an added comma in the original German of the second sentence quoted above (i.e. in the *Imago* version) which—because it does not correspond to English grammar—is not represented in the translation ('*dem Menschen der Vorzeit, zuschreiben dürfen*').]

[23] [This paragraph is replaced by the following one in the *Imago* version:]

What the attitude of prehistoric man was towards death is, of course, only known to us by inferences and constructions, but I believe that these methods have furnished us with fairly trustworthy conclusions.

[24] [This sentence is deleted in the *Imago* version, and the first two sentences in the paragraph are replaced by the following:]

Primaeval man took up a very remarkable attitude **towards** death. It was far from consistent; it was indeed most contradictory.

'DEATH AND US' 21

On the one hand, he took death seriously, accepted that it meant the annihilation of life and made use of it in that sense; on the other hand he denied it, diminished it to nothing. How is this possible? It arose from the fact that he took up a radically different attitude towards the death of other people, of strangers, of enemies, and towards his own. He had no objection towards someone else's death; he understood it as annihilation and craved to bring it about. Primaeval man was a passionate creature and more cruel and more malignant than the other animals.[25] He was not held back from killing and devouring his own species by an instinct of the sort claimed for most predatory animals. He liked to kill, and killed as a matter of course.[26]

Hence the primaeval history of mankind is filled with murder. Even *to-day*, the history of the world learned at school by

---

[25] [The last five sentences are slightly modified and reduced to the following four sentences in the *Imago* version:]
On the one hand, he took death seriously, **recognized it as** the **termination** of life and made use of it in that sense; **but** on the other hand he **also** denied **death and reduced** it to nothing. **This contradiction** arose from the fact that he took up radically different attitudes towards the death of other people, of strangers, of enemies, and towards his own. He had no objection towards someone else's death; **it meant the** annihilation **of someone he hated, and primitive man had no scruples about** bringing it about. **He** was **no doubt** a **very** passionate creature and more cruel and more malignant than **other** animals.

[Note that in the original German, the word 'but' (*aber*) was added after the semi-colon in the first sentence, which is not reflected in Strachey's translation (*S.E.*, *14*, 292).]

[26] [The last two sentences in the paragraph are reversed and modified as follows in the *Imago* version:]
He liked to kill, and killed as a matter of course. **The instinct which is said to restrain other animals** from killing and devouring his own species **need not be attributed to him.**

[Note that the words 'his own species' correspond to different German words in the first and second versions ('*seiner eigenen Art*' and '*der gleichen Art*', respectively). This change is difficult to translate, and is not reflected in the translation of the second version quoted above (i.e. Strachey's *S.E.* translation).

Note also that the term 'instinct'—in both versions—corresponds to the German '*Instinkt*' rather than '*Trieb*' (cf. *S.E.*, *1*, xxv).]

our children is essentially a series of murders of peoples. The vague sense of guilt to which mankind has been subject since the very beginning, and which in some religions has been condensed into the doctrine of *primal guilt*, of *original sin*, is very probably the outcome of a blood-guilt that the men of prehistory brought upon themselves.[27] The Christian doctrine still enables us to guess what this guilt consisted in. If the Son of God was obliged to sacrifice his life to redeem mankind from original sin, then by the law of talion, the requital of like by like, that sin was a killing, a murder. Nothing else could call for the sacrifice of a life for its expiation. And if the original sin was an offence against God the Father, the primal crime of mankind must have been a parricide, the killing of the primal father of the primitive human horde, whose mnemic image was later transfigured into a deity. In my book *Totem and Taboo* (1912–13), I have tried to collect the evidence for this interpretation of primal guilt.[28]

---

[27] [The first sentence in this paragraph remains unchanged in the *Imago* version, but the second and third sentences are very slightly modified:]
Even *to-day*, the history of the world **which our children learn at school** is essentially a series of murders of peoples. The **obscure** sense of guilt to which mankind has been subject since **prehistoric times**, and which in some religions has been condensed into the doctrine of *primal guilt*, of original sin, is **probably** the outcome of a blood-guilt **incurred by prehistoric man**.

[Note that the word '*Urschuld*' ('primal guilt') is emphasized in both versions, but this is not reflected in Strachey's translation of the *Imago* version (*S.E.*, *14*, 292).]

[28] [The last of the aforegoing five sentences is moved and expanded in the *Imago* version, and the second sentence is very slightly modified; the rest of the paragraph remains unchanged:]
In my book *Totem and Taboo* (1912–13) I have, following clues given by Robertson Smith, Atkinson and Charles Darwin, tried to guess the nature of this primal guilt, and I believe, too, that the Christian doctrine of to-day enables us to deduce it. If the Son of God was obliged to sacrifice his life to redeem mankind from original sin, then by the law of talion, the requital of like by like, that sin **must have been** a killing, a murder. Nothing else could call for the sacrifice of a life for its expiation. And if the original sin was an offence against God

Incidentally, let me point out that the doctrine of original sin is not a Christian innovation; it is a part of the primal belief that has continued for ages in subterranean religious currents. Judaism has carefully pushed aside these dark memories of mankind, and perhaps for this very reason has disqualified itself as a world religion.[29]

Let us return to primaeval man and to his attitude towards death. We have heard what his position was on the death of strangers. His own death was certainly just as unimaginable and unreal for him as it is for any one of us *to-day*.[30] But there was for him one case in which the two opposite attitudes towards death collided and came into conflict with each other; and this case became highly important and productive of far-reaching consequences. It occurred when primaeval man saw someone who belonged to him die—his wife, his child, his friend—whom he certainly loved as we love ours, for love is definitely no younger than the lust to kill. Then he learned that one can die, for each of these loved ones was, after all, a part of his own ego, but on the other hand, in each of these loved persons there was also, after all, something of the stranger.[31]

---

the Father, the primal crime of mankind must have been a parricide, the killing of the primal father of the primitive human horde, whose mnemic image was later transfigured into a deity.

[Also, the following footnote is appended at the end:]

Cf. *Totem and Taboo*, Essay IV [*S.E.*, *13*, 146ff.].

[Note that the word 'if' in the last sentence was omitted in Strachey's translation (*S.E.*, *14*, 293)—no doubt by typographer's error.]

[29] [This paragraph, and the first two sentences of the next, are deleted in the *Imago* version.]

[30] [In the *Imago* version, this sentence, which becomes the first in the new paragraph, reads as follows:]

His own death was certainly just as unimaginable and unreal for **primaeval man** as it is for any one of us today.

[Here there is also an additional comma in the *Imago* version of the original German for which there is no equivalent in English grammatical usage.]

[31] [The first of the aforegoing three sentences remains unchanged in the *Imago* version, but the next two are modified and expanded into the following three:]

It occurred when primaeval man saw someone who belonged to him

According to the laws of psychology, which are valid to this day, and which governed us far more widely in primaeval times, these loved ones were, simultaneously, also enemies and strangers who had aroused in him some degree of hostile feeling.[32] Philosophers have declared that the intellectual enigma presented to primaeval man by the picture of death forced him to reflection, and thus became the starting-point of all speculation. I should like to limit and correct this proposition.[33] What released the spirit of enquiry in man was not the intellectual enigma, and not every death, but the conflict of feeling at the

---

die—his wife, his child, his friend—whom he **undoubtedly** loved as we love ours, for love **cannot be much** younger than the lust to kill. Then, **in his pain, he was forced to learn** that one can die, **too, oneself, and his whole being revolted against the admission;** each of these loved ones was, after all, a part of his own **beloved** ego. On the other hand, **deaths such as these pleased him as well, since in each of the** loved persons **there was** also something of the stranger.

[Note that in the German original of the second version, the words '*denn*' ('for'—in the phrase '**for** each of these loved ones was') and '*aber*' ('but'—in the sentence beginning '**but** on the other hand') are deleted. This is not reflected in Strachey's translation (*S.E.*, *14*, 293).

Regarding the use of the term 'ego' in the second sentence of Strachey's translation (quoted above), see *S.E.*, *24*, 448.]

[32] [This sentence is modified and expanded into the following two in the *Imago* version:]
The law of ambivalence of feeling, which to this day **governs our emotional relations with those whom we love most, certainly had a very much wider validity** in primaeval times. **Thus** these **beloved dead had also been** enemies and strangers who had aroused in him some degree of hostile feeling.

[Also, the following footnote is appended at the end:]
See *Totem and Taboo*, **Essay II** [*S.E.*, *13*, 60ff.].

[33] [The first sentence in this paragraph remains unchanged in the *Imago* version, but the second sentence is expanded into the following three:]
I believe that here the philosophers are thinking too philosophically, and giving too little consideration to the motives that were primarily operative. I should like **therefore** to limit and correct **their** assertion. **In my view, primaeval man must have triumphed beside the body of his slain enemy, without being led to rack his brains about the enigma of life and death.**

death of loved yet alien and hated persons. Of this conflict of feeling psychology was the first offspring.³⁴ Primaeval man could no longer deny death, in his pain he had, after all, partially experienced it; but he was nevertheless loath to acknowledge it, because he could not think of himself as dead. So he devised a compromise: he conceded the fact of death, but denied that it was annihilation—the fate that he had wished upon his enemy all the same.³⁵ It was beside the body of someone he loved that he made up spirits, that he invented the division of the individual into a body and a soul—originally several souls. In remembering the dead he created in himself the notion of other forms of life, for which death is but the beginning, and the conception of a life continuing after apparent death.³⁶ These subsequent existences were at first no more than appendages

---

³⁴ [The last two sentences remain unchanged in the *Imago* version.]

³⁵ [The last two sentences are slightly modified in the *Imago* version:] Man could no longer **keep** death **at a distance, for** he had **tasted it** in his pain **about the dead**; but he was nevertheless **unwilling** to acknowledge it, **for** he could not **conceive** of himself as dead. So he devised a compromise: he conceded the fact of **his own** death **as well**, but denied **it the significance of** annihilation—**a significance which he had no motive for denying where the death of** his enemy **was concerned.**

[However, in the original German, the word 'his' in '**his** pain' and '**his** enemy' is replaced by the word 'the' (i.e. '**the** pain' and '**the** enemy); the word 'he' in '**he** conceded' is deleted; and the word 'but' in '**but** denied' is moved (i.e. '**but** denied it' becomes 'denied it **however**'). These minor and insignificant changes, which cannot be satisfactorily reflected in English grammatical usage, are not reflected in Strachey's translation (as quoted above).]

³⁶ [The last two sentences are modified and expanded as follows in the *Imago* version:]
It was beside the body of someone he loved that he **invented** spirits, **and his sense of guilt at the satisfaction mingled with his sorrow turned these new-born spirits into evil demons that had to be dreaded. The** [physical] **changes brought about by death suggested to him** the division of the individual into a body and a soul—originally several—**and in this way his train of thought ran parallel with the process of disintegration which sets in with death. His persisting memory of** the dead **became the basis for assuming** other forms of life

to the existence that death had brought to a close—shadowy, empty of content and valued at little; they still bore with themselves the character of wretched makeshifts.[37] Allow me to recite to you the words of our great poet Heinrich Heine, whereby—in full agreement, incidentally, with the ancient Homer—the dead Achilles gave expression to his low opinion of the life after death:

> Der kleinste lebendige Philister
> Zu Stuckert am Neckar
> Viel glücklicher ist er
> Als ich, der Pelide, der tote Held,
> Der Schattenfürst in der Unterwelt.[38]

Only later did religions succeed in turning this after-life into the more desirable, the truly valid one, and in reducing the life

---

and gave him the conception of a life continuing after apparent death.

[Note that in the German original of the *Imago* version, the sentence ending with the words 'a body and a soul—originally several souls' is merged into the following sentence: 'a body and a soul—originally several**—and i**n this way'. Strachey's translation does not reflect this (*S.E.*, *14*, 294).]

[37] [This sentence is slightly modified, and begins a new paragraph, in the *Imago* version:]

These subsequent existences were at first no more than appendages to the existence which death had brought to a close—shadowy, empty of content and valued at little **until later times**; they still bore **the** character of wretched makeshifts.

[38] [Literally: 'The smallest living Philistine at Stuckert-am-Neckar is far happier than I, the son of Peleus, the dead hero, the shadow-prince of the underworld.' These, the closing lines of 'Der Scheidende'—one of Heine's very last poems—are introduced differently in the *Imago* version:]

We may recall the answer made to Odysseus by the soul of Achilles:

> **'For of old, when thou wast alive, we Argives honoured thee even as the gods, and now that thou art here, thou rulest mightily over the dead. Wherefore grieve not at all that thou art dead, Achilles.'**
> **So I spoke, and he straightaway made answer and said:**
> **'Nay, seek not to speak soothingly to me of death, glorious Odysseus. I should choose, so I might live on earth, to serve as the hireling of another, of some portionless man whose livelihood was**

which is ended by death to a mere preparation. After this, it was merely consistent to extend life backwards into the past, to form the notion of earlier existences, of reincarnation and of the transmigration of souls, all with the purpose of depriving death of its meaning as the termination of life.[39] It is very remarkable that our Holy Scriptures have taken no account of this human need for a guarantee of continued existence. On the contrary, at one point it is said: 'Only the living praise God.'[40] I believe—and you certainly know more about it than I do—that different stances have been taken on the doctrine of immortality in popular Jewish religion and in the literature connected with the Holy Scriptures. But I would like to include this point too amongst those factors that prevented the Jewish religion from

---

but small, rather than to be lord over all the dead that have perished.'
(*Odyssey XI*, 484–491. [Trans. A. T. Murray.])
Or in Heine's powerful and bitter parody:

[39] [The last two sentences are very slightly modified in the *Imago* version:]

It was only later that religions succeeded in **representing** this after-life **as** the more desirable, the truly valid one, and in reducing the life which is ended by death to a mere preparation. After this, it was **no more than** consistent to extend life backwards into the past **as well**, to form the notion of earlier existences, of **the transmigration of souls** and of **reincarnation**, all with the purpose of depriving death of its meaning as the termination of life.

[Three further insignificant modifications in the second version cannot be meaningfully reflected in English translation. In the original German, the words 'desirable' and 'valid' are spelled '*wertvolleren*' and '*vollgültigen*' in the first version, but '*wertvollere*' and '*vollgültige*' in the second; and the phrase 'to extend life backwards into the past' is equivalent to '*in die Vergangenheit hinein verlängerte*' in the first version and '*in die Vergangenheit verlängerte*' in the second. Also, note that in the original German of the second version the word '*auch*' ('as well') is inserted into the second sentence, which is not reflected in Strachey's translation (*S.E.*, *14*, 295).]

[40] [This is not a direct quotation from the Scriptures. Cf., however, *Psalms* cxv, 17, 'The dead praise not the Lord, neither any that go down into silence'; and *Isaiah* xxxviii, 18–19, 'For the grave cannot praise thee, death cannot celebrate thee: they that go down into the pit cannot hope for thy truth. The living, the living, he shall praise thee'.]

taking the place of the other ancient religions after their decline.[41]

What came into existence beside the body of the loved one was not only the doctrine of the soul and the belief in immortality, but also the sense of guilt, the fear of death and the earliest ethical commandments.[42] The sense of guilt arose out of the contradictory feeling towards the deceased and the fear of death from the identification with him. From the logical viewpoint, however, this latter was of little consequence, for disbelief in one's own death was not done away with all the same. And we modern men are still no closer to solving the paradox.[43] The oldest, and to this day the most important commandment imposed by ethics at that time was: 'Thou shalt not kill.' It was acquired in relation to dead people who were loved, and it was gradually extended to strangers, to those who were not loved, and finally even to enemies.[44]

---

[41] [The last four sentences of this paragraph are omitted in the *Imago* version, where they are replaced by the following one:]
So early did the denial of death, which we have described [footnote 9] **as a 'conventional and cultural attitude', have its origin.**

[42] [This sentence is modified as follows in the *Imago* version:]
What came into existence beside the body of the loved one was not only the doctrine of the soul, the belief in immortality **and a powerful source of** man's sense of guilt, **but also** the earliest ethical commandments.

[43] [The last three sentences are deleted in the *Imago* version.]

[44] [The last two sentences are slightly modified in the *Imago* version:]
The **first** and most important **prohibition made** by **the awakening conscience** was: **Thou shalt not kill.** It was acquired in relation to dead people who were loved, **as a reaction against the satisfaction of the hatred hidden behind the grief for them;** and it was gradually extended to **strangers who** were not loved, and finally even to enemies.

[Note that the emphasis and the inverted commas in 'Thou shalt not kill' are dropped. The latter change is not reflected in Strachey's translation (*S.E., 14,* 295).]

Incidentally, modern Jewish scholarship suggests that—since the Hebrew stem *r-ts-h* applies only to illegal killing—the first commandment should be translated, 'Thou shalt not **murder**', rather than 'Thou shalt not **kill**'. This is not reflected in the present translation as Freud, in the original German, used the conventional *töten.*

'DEATH AND US' 29

At this point I would like to tell you a peculiar fact. In a certain sense primaeval man really still exists; he is represented to us by the primitive savage—or at least, the primitive savage is closest to him. Now you might be inclined to adopt the view that these primitives, the savage Australians, Tierra del Fuegans, Bushmen, etc., are remorseless murderers. But remember, the savage is more sensitive in this regard than civilized man—at least until he succumbs to the influence of civilization. After the happy conclusion of the world war that is currently raging, each one of the victorious German soldiers will hurry home to his wife and his children, unchecked and undisturbed by thoughts of the enemies that he killed, be it at close quarters or at long range. But savages who return victorious from the war-path may not set foot in their villages or see their wives till they have atoned for the murders they committed in war by penances that are often long and tedious. You might say: 'Yes, the savage is still superstitious, he goes in fear of the avenging spirits of the slain.' But the spirits of his slain enemy are nothing but the expression of his bad conscience about his blood-guilt.[45]

---

[45] [This paragraph is revised and reshuffled as follows in the *Imago* version:]

This final extension of the commandment is no longer experienced by civilized man. When the furious struggle of the current war has been decided each one of the victorious **fighters** will **return** home **joyfully** to his wife **and children**, unchecked and undisturbed by thoughts of the enemies **he has killed whether** at close quarters or at long range. **It is worthy of note that the** primitive **races which still survive in the world, and are undoubtedly closer than we are to** primaeval man, **act differently in this respect, or did until they came under** the influence of **our civilization. Savages**—Australians, **Bushmen, Tierra del Fuegans—are far from being** remorseless murderers; **when they** return victorious from the war-path they may not set foot in their villages or **touch** their wives till they have atoned for the murders they committed in war by penances which are often long and tedious. **It is easy, of course, to attribute this to their superstition: the savage still** goes in fear of the avenging spirits of the slain. But the spirits of his slain enemy are nothing but the expression of his bad conscience about his blood-guilt; **behind this superstition there lies**

Let me tarry a moment longer on this the oldest of ethical commandments: 'Thou shalt not kill'. Its early appearance and its urgency alike permit us to draw an important conclusion. The claim has been made that an instinctual [*instinktiver*] aversion to bloodshed is deeply implanted within us. Pious souls like to believe it. Now, we could easily put this claim to the test. We have really good cases of instinctual [*instinktiver*], inherited aversions of this sort at our disposal.

Let me transport you to one of our lovely health-resorts in the South. There, there are vineyards with magnificent grapes. In these vineyards there are snakes, too, thick black ones called Aesculapian snakes (completely harmless animals, incidentally). There are also notices of prohibition in these vineyards. We read one of these notices, upon which is written: 'It is strictly prohibited for guests of the resort to stick the head or the tail of an Aesculapian snake into their mouths.' Wouldn't you say, 'What a senseless and unnecessary prohibition. No such thing would occur to anyone anyway.' You would be right. We also read other notices that warn against the picking of grapes. We would consider this prohibition more justified.—No, don't let us lead ourselves astray. We possess no instinctual [*instinktiven*] aversion to bloodshed. We are the descendants of an endless series of generations of murderers. The lust for killing is infixed in our blood, and soon, perhaps, we shall be able to track it down in other places too [p. 36].[46]

---

concealed a vein of ethical sensitiveness which has been lost by us civilized men.

[Note that the word 'civilization' in the third sentence of the paragraph is equivalent to the German '*Zivilisation*' in the first version and '*Kultur*' in the second. On the problem of the translation of these terms, see Strachey (*S.E.*, *21*, 4) and Bettelheim (1982, pp. 99–100).]

[46] [The last two paragraphs are deleted in the *Imago* version and replaced by the following one:]

Pious souls, **no doubt, who would** like to believe **that our nature is remote from any contact with what is evil and base, will not fail to use the early appearance and the urgency of the prohibition against murder as the basis for gratifying conclusions as to the strength of the ethical impulses which must have been** implanted **in us. Unfortunately this argument proves even more the opposite view. So**

We now leave primaeval man, and turn to our own mental life. Perhaps you are aware that we are in possession of an investigative procedure which enables us to discover what is happening in the deeper strata of the mind, hidden from consciousness—that is to say, of a sort of *under-water psychology*. What, we therefore ask, is the attitude of our unconscious towards the problem of death? And now we come to what you won't believe [p. 20], although it is no longer new to you for I described it to you a moment ago. Our unconscious, you see, adopts exactly the same attitude to death as the man of prehistoric times. In this respect, as in many others, primaeval man survives unchanged in us. The unconscious in us, then, does not believe in its own death. It is compelled to behave as if it were immortal. This may even be the secret of heroism. The rational grounds for heroism admittedly rest on a judgement that the subject's own life cannot be so precious as certain other general and abstract goods. But more frequent, in my view, is the impulsive or instinctive [*instinktive*] heroism that behaves like a guarantee embodied in the well-known cry of Steinklopferhans:[47] 'Nothing can happen to *me*'—which consists, therefore, in simply abandoning oneself to the unconscious belief in immortality. The fear of death, from which we suffer far oftener than we know, is an illogical contradiction of

---

powerful a prohibition can only be directed against an equally powerful impulse. What no human soul desires stands in no need of prohibition; it is excluded automatically. The very emphasis laid on the commandment 'Thou shalt not kill' makes it certain that we sprang from an endless series of generations of murderers, who had the lust for killing in their blood, as , perhaps, we ourselves have to-day. Mankind's ethical strivings, whose strength and significance we need not in the least depreciate, were acquired in the course of man's history; since then they have become, though unfortunately only in a very variable amount, the inherited property of contemporary man.

[Also, the following footnote is appended to the phrase 'What no human soul desires stands in no need of prohibition':]

Cf. Frazer's brilliant argument quoted in my *Totem and Taboo* [*S.E.*, *13*, 123.]

[47] ['Hans the Stone-Breaker'—a character in a comedy by the Viennese dramatist Ludwig Anzengruber (1839–89).]

this confidence. It was, incidentally, by no means that initially, and is usually the outcome of a sense of guilt.[48]

On the other hand, for strangers and for enemies we do acknowledge death, and make use of it against them as did primaeval man. The only distinction is that we no longer actu-

---

[48] [This paragraph is somewhat modified in the *Imago* version:]
Let us now leave primaeval man, and turn to **the unconscious in** our own mental life. **Here we depend entirely upon the psycho-analytic method of investigation, the only one which reaches to such depths.** What, **we ask**, is the attitude of our unconscious towards the problem of death? **The answer must be: almost exactly the same as that of primaeval man.** In this respect, as in many others, **the man of prehistoric times** survives unchanged in **our unconscious. Our unconscious**, then, does not believe in its own death; **it behaves** as if it were immortal. **What we call our 'unconscious'—the deepest strata of our minds, made up of instinctual impulses [*Triebregungen*]—knows nothing that is negative, and no negation; in it contradictories coincide. For that reason it does not know its own death, for to that we can only give a negative content. Thus there is nothing instinctual [*Triebhaftes*] in us which responds to a belief in death.** This may even be the secret of heroism. The rational grounds for heroism **rest** on a judgement that the subject's own life cannot be so precious as certain **abstract** and **general** goods. But more frequent, in my view, is the **instinctive [*instinktive*] and impulsive** heroism which **knows no such reasons, and simply flouts danger in the spirit of Anzengruber's** *Steinklopferhans*: *Nothing can happen to* me. **Or else those reasons only serve to clear away those hesitations which might hold back the heroic reaction that corresponds to the unconscious.** The fear of death, **which dominates us** oftener than we **ourselves** know, is **on the other hand something secondary**, and is usually the outcome of a sense of guilt.

[Note that the word 'simply' (*einfach*) in the phrase 'and simply flouts danger' and the word 'ourselves' (*selbst*) in 'oftener than we ourselves know' are overlooked in Strachey's translation, whilst the inverted commas in 'Nothing can happen to *me*', which should have been dropped, are retained, and the emphasis which should have been added, is not (cf. *S.E.*, *14*, 350–351). There is a further change which *could* not be reflected in Strachey's translation as there is no equivalent in English grammatical usage: the phrase '*und wenden uns dem eigenen Seelenleben zu*' ('and turn to our own mental life') in the first sentence of the B'nai B'rith version, becomes '*und wenden **wir** uns dem . . .*' in the *Imago* version.]

ally bring about the killing; we merely think it and wish it. But if you accept this so-called psychical reality as valid, then you could say: today, in our unconscious, we are still all a gang of murderers. Daily and hourly in our unspoken thoughts we get rid of anyone who stands in our way, of anyone who has offended or injured us. The expression: 'Devil take him!', which comes to people's lips so often in the form of a mild interjection and which, in truth, implies 'Death take him!', is powerfully serious for our unconscious.[49] Indeed our unconscious will murder even for trifles; like the ancient Athenian code of Draco, it knows no other punishment for crime than death. And this has a certain consistency, for every injury to our almighty and autocratic ego is at bottom a crime of *lèse-majesté*.[50] How very fortunate that all these wicked wishes do not possess any power. Otherwise, the human race would long since have died out; neither the best and wisest among the men nor the loveliest and fairest women would have survived. No, here too, don't let us lead ourselves astray; we are

---

[49] [Up to this point, the present paragraph is revised as follows in the *Imago* version:]

On the other hand, for strangers and for enemies we do acknowledge death, and **consign them to it quite as readily and unhesitatingly** as did primaeval man. **There is, it is true, a** distinction **here which will be pronounced decisive so far as real life is concerned. Our unconscious does not carry out** the killing; it merely **thinks** it and **wishes** it. But **it would be wrong so completely to undervalue this** *psychical* **reality as compared with** *factual* **reality. It is significant and momentous enough.** In our **unconscious impulses** we **daily and hourly** get rid of anyone who stands in our way, of anyone who has offended **and** injured us. The expression 'Devil take him!', which **so often** comes to people's lips in **joking anger** and which **really means** 'Death take him!', is **in our unconscious a serious and powerful death-wish.**

[Note that the words 'psychical' and 'factual' are not emphasized (as they should be) in Strachey's translation, and that the word 'or' (*oder*) in the phrase 'offended or injured us', which should have been changed to 'and' (*uns beleidigt und geschädigt*), is erroneously left as it is (cf. *S.E.*, *14*, 297).]

[50] [The above two sentences are left unchanged in the *Imago* version, apart from the insertion of a comma at the beginning: 'Indeed, our unconscious . . .'.]

still the murderers today that our forefathers were in primaeval times.[51]

I can say all of this to you quite calmly because I know, of course, that you don't believe it. You are more inclined to believe your consciousness, which rejects such possibilities as calumnies. For that reason, I have no choice but to hold up before you the fact that there have been poets and thinkers who knew nothing of our *psycho-analysis* and yet declared similar things. I offer but a single example![52] At one point in his works—I can no longer locate where—J. J. Rousseau interrupts himself to discuss a remarkable question with his reader. 'Imagine', he says, 'that there is a mandarin in Peking' (in those days Peking was very much further from Paris than it is today) 'whose death would bring you great profit, and you could kill him—without leaving Paris, without the possibility of any evidence pointing to your deed, of course—by a mere act of will.

---

[51] [The last three sentences are condensed into a new paragraph in the *Imago* version:]

And so, if we are to be judged by our unconscious wishful impulses, we ourselves are, like primaeval man, a gang of murderers. It is fortunate that all **these wishes** do not possess **the potency that was attributed to them in primaeval times; in the cross-fire of mutual curses mankind** would long since have **perished,** the best and wisest **of** men **and** the loveliest and fairest **of** women **with the rest.**

[Also, the following footnote is appended to the phrase, 'the potency that was attributed to them in primaeval times':]

See *Totem and Taboo*, Essay IV [S.E., 13, 85f.].

[52] [The opening four sentences of the present paragraph correspond to the following four, which form a separate paragraph in the *Imago* version:]

Psycho-analysis finds as a rule no credence among laymen for assertions such as these. They reject them as calumnies **which are confuted by conscious experience, and they adroitly overlook the faint indications by which even the unconscious is apt to betray itself to** consciousness. **It is therefore relevant to point out that many** thinkers who **could not have been influenced by psychoanalysis have quite definitely accused our unspoken thoughts of being ready, heedless of the prohibition against murder, to get rid of anything which stands in our way. From many examples of this I will choose one that has become famous:**

Are you sure that you would not do it?' Now, I do not doubt that many among the dear Brethren could rightfully give the assurance that they would not do it. But on the whole I would still not like to be the mandarin; I do not think that any life-assurance company would accept him.[53]

I can convey the same unpleasant truth to you in a form that could even give you pleasure. I know that you all like to be told jokes, and I hope that you have not been too much preoccupied with the problem of where the satisfaction in jokes comes from. There is a certain class of jokes that we call *cynical*; they are not the worst or weakest of jokes. I can reveal to you that part of the secret of these jokes is to dress up a hidden or unacknowledged truth—something that is, in and of itself, offensive—in such a way that one is actually able to enjoy it. By way of certain formal arrangements, you are compelled to laugh, your judgement is disarmed, and the truth which would otherwise have been tracked down is smuggled through. You know, for instance, the story about the man who is delivered of a funeral-notice whilst in company, which he puts in his pocket, unread. 'Wouldn't you rather have a look to see who it is that has died?', someone asks him. 'What for?', he answers, 'It's fine by me no matter who it is'. Or the one about the husband who says, regarding his wife: 'If one of us dies, I shall move to Paris.' These are cynical jokes, and they would not be possible unless they contained an unacknowledged truth. In jest—it is well known—one may even tell the truth.[54]

---

[53] [This paragraph is somewhat modified and condensed in the *Imago* version:]

In *Le Père Goriot*, Balzac alludes to a passage in the works of J. J. Rousseau where that author asks the reader what he would do if—without leaving Paris **and** of course without **being discovered**—he could kill, **with** great profit **to himself, an old** mandarin in Peking by a mere act of will. **Rousseau implies that he would not give much for the life of that dignitary. '*Tuer son mandarin*' has become a proverbial phrase for this secret readiness, present even in modern man.**

[54] [This paragraph is much abridged in the *Imago* version:]

There are a whole number of cynical jokes and anecdotes which reveal the same tendency—such, for instance, as the words attrib-

My dear brethren! Yet another complete correspondence between primaeval man and our unconscious. Exactly as it was for him, it is also the case for our unconscious that the two currents, the one that acknowledges death as annihilation and the other that denies it as unreal, collide and come into conflict. This case is the same as in primal ages: the death, or the risk of death, of someone we love, a parent or a partner in marriage, a brother or sister, child or dear friend. These loved ones are on the one hand an inner possession, elements of our own ego; but on the other hand they are partly strangers, even enemies. With the exception of only a very few situations, there adheres to the tenderest and most intimate of our relationships a small portion of hostility which excites an unconscious death-wish. But the conflict between the two currents does not lead any longer to the doctrine of the soul and to ethics, but to *neurosis*, which affords us deep insight into normal mental life as well. The frequent occurrence of exaggerated worry among relatives and of entirely baseless self-reproaches after deaths in the family has opened our eyes to the extent and importance of these deeply hidden death-wishes.[55]

---

uted to the husband: 'If one of us **two** dies, I shall move to Paris.' **Such** cynical **jokes would** not be possible unless they contained an unacknowledged truth **which could not be admitted if it were expressed seriously and without disguise**. In jest—it is well known—one may even tell the truth.

[55] [This paragraph is only slightly modified in the *Imago* version:]
Just as for primaeval man, **so also for** our unconscious, **there is one** case **in which the two opposing attitudes towards death**, the one which acknowledges **it** as **the** annihilation **of life** and the other which denies it as unreal, collide and come into conflict. This case is the same as in primal ages: the death, or the risk of death, of someone we love, a parent or a partner in marriage, a brother or sister, child or **beloved** friend. These loved ones are on the one hand an inner possession, **components** of our own ego; but on the other hand they are partly strangers, even enemies. With the exception of only a very few situations, there adheres to the tenderest and most intimate of our **love-relations** a small portion of hostility which **can excite** an unconscious death-wish. But the conflict **due to ambivalence** does not **now, as it did then,** lead to the doctrine of the soul and to ethics, but to **neurosis**,

I will not sketch this aspect of the picture any further. You are probably becoming horrified—mistakenly, in fact. Here, once again, Nature has acted more skilfully than we imagine. It certainly does not occur to us that it could be an advantage thus to couple love and hate. But Nature, by making use of this pair of opposites, forces us to keep love ever vigilant and to revitalize it, in this way to safeguard it from the hate that lurks behind it. It might be said that we owe the fairest flowerings of love to the *reaction* against the cravings of the lust to kill that we sense within us.[56]

---

which affords us deep insight into normal mental life as well. **How often have physicians who practise psycho-analysis had to deal with the symptom of** exaggerated worry **over the well-being of** relatives, **or with** entirely **unfounded** self-reproaches after **the death of a loved person. The study of such phenomena has left them in no doubt about** the extent and importance of **unconscious** death-wishes.

[Note that the phrase 'a parent or a partner in marriage' corresponds to the German '*eines Eltern- oder Gattenteile*' in the first version and '*eines Eltern- oder Gattenteiles*' in the second. This minor difference cannot, once again, be represented in English translation. Similarly, note that Strachey inserted two 'a's in the phrase 'a child and a dear friend'. Also note that here he translated '**lieben** *Freundes*' ('**beloved** friend') as '**dear** friend' (*S.E.*, *14*, 298; cf. footnote 9 above).]

[56] [This paragraph is somewhat modified in the *Imago* version:]
The layman feels an extraordinary horror at the possibility of such feelings, and takes this aversion as a legitimate ground for disbelief in the assertions of psycho-analysis. Without justification, I think. No depreciation of feelings of love is intended, and there is in fact none. It is indeed foreign to our intelligence as well as to our feelings thus to couple love and hate; but Nature, by making use of this pair of opposites, **contrives** to keep love ever vigilant and **fresh, so as to guard** it **against** the hate which lurks behind it. It might be said that we owe the fairest flowerings of **our** love to the *reaction* against the **hostile impulse** which we sense within us.

[Note that the English 'we owe' in the last sentence corresponds to the German '*verdanken wir*' in the first version and '*danken wir*' in the second—an insignificant change which cannot be reflected in translation. Note also that Strachey neglected to emphasize the word 'reaction' in his translation of this last sentence (*S.E.*, *14*, 299).]

To sum up: our unconscious is just as inaccessible to the idea of our own death, just as murderously inclined towards strangers, just as divided (that is, ambivalent) towards those we love, as was primaeval man. But how far have we moved from this primal state in our cultural attitude towards death![57]

And now let us look once again at what the war does to us. It strips us of the later accretions of civilization, and lays bare the primal man in each of us. It compels us once more to be heroes who will not believe in their own death; it stamps strangers as enemies, whose death is to be brought about or desired; it tells us to disregard the death of those we love.[58] Thus it makes all of our cultural death-conventions untenable.[59] But war cannot be swept away. For as long as the differences in the conditions of existence among nations and their mutual repulsion are so great, for so long there are bound to be wars. The question then arises: Is it not we who should give in, who should adapt ourselves to the war? Should we not confess that in our civilized attitude towards death we are living psychologically beyond our means, and should we not rather turn back and recognize the truth? Would it not be better to give death the place in reality and in our thoughts that is its due, and to give a little more prominence to the unconscious attitude towards death that we have hitherto so carefully suppressed?[60] I cannot make this

---

[57] [This paragraph remains unchanged in the *Imago* version, except that the words 'our cultural attitude' in the last sentence become '**the conventional and** cultural attitude'. Note, however, that Strachey mistakenly translated the 'the' (*der*) in this latter sentence as 'our' (*S.E., 14*, 299).]

[58] [Up to this point, the present paragraph remains unchanged in the *Imago* version, excepting that the opening sentence becomes, '**It is easy to see how war impinges on this dichotomy**', and the phrase 'heroes who will not believe in their own death' becomes 'heroes who **cannot** believe . . .' (cf. *S.E., 14*, 299).].

[59] [This sentence is deleted in the *Imago* version, and the following two sentences are combined and modified as follows:]
But war cannot be **abolished; so** long as the conditions of existence among nations **are so different** and their mutual repulsion **so violent, there** are bound to be wars.

[60] [The last three sentences are slightly modified in the *Imago* version:]

'DEATH AND US' 39

appeal to you as if it were an advance to higher achievement, for indeed it is, rather, a backward step—a regression. But it would definitely contribute towards making life more tolerable for us once again; and to tolerate life is indeed the first duty of all living things. At school we heard the old Latin saying that went: '*Si vis pacem, para bellum*'. If you want to preserve peace, arm for war. For our present-day needs we could alter it:

'Si vis vitam, para mortem'.

If you want to endure life, prepare yourself for death.[61]

The question then arises: Is it not we who should give in, who should **adapt to** the war? Should we not confess that in our civilized attitude towards death we are **once again** living psychologically beyond our means, and should we not rather turn back and recognize the truth? Would it not be better to give death the place in reality and in our thoughts which is its due, and to give to the unconscious attitude towards death which we have hitherto so carefully suppressed **a little more prominence**?

[Two of these changes are not reflected in Strachey's translation: namely; the deletion of the word '*uns*' (ourselves) in the first sentence (it is replaced by '*sich*' which is silent in English); and the shifting of the phrase '*ein wenig mehr . . . hervorzukehren*' ('to give . . . a little more prominence') to the end of the third sentence (cf. *S.E.*, *14*, 299).]

[61] [These closing sentences are slightly expanded and are set differently in the *Imago* version:]
This hardly seems an advance to higher achievement, **but** rather **in some respects** a backward step—a regression; **but it has the advantage of taking the truth more into account, and of** making life more tolerable for us once again. To tolerate life **remains, after all,** the first duty of all living **beings. Illusion becomes valueless if it makes this harder for us.**
   We recall the old **saying**:
      Si vis pacem, para bellum.
   (If you want to preserve peace, arm for war.)
   It would be in keeping with the times to alter it:
      Si vis vitam, para mortem.
   (If you want to endure life, prepare yourself for death.)
[Note the deletion of the inverted commas, the new arrangement of the type, and the addition of brackets at the end. The latter two changes are not reflected in Strachey's translation (*S.E.*, *14*, 299–300).]

EDITOR'S COMMENT

David Meghnagi

What we are presenting here is the text, whose original title was *'Wir und der Tod'*, of a lecture held by Freud on 16 February 1915, at the Viennese branch of the Jewish movement B'nai B'rith, which he joined two years after its foundation in September of 1897.

As he himself was to acknowledge many years later, in 1926, on the occasion of celebrations for his seventieth birthday, it was at the B'nai B'rith that Freud gave his first lectures and popularizing talks on psychoanalysis. When the rest of the world still ignored and showed hostility to him, it was 'among his Jewish brethren' that he found the warmth and support necessary to pursue his revolutionary work. (For a complete list of Freud's lectures to the B'nai B'rith and for a reconstructed summary of their contents, see D. B. Klein, 1981, pp. 155–165.)

The years during which Freud was a member of B'nai B'rith were full of significance for Jewish society and for the rise of psychoanalysis itself. In 1897, Karl Lueger, the social Christian antisemite, was elected mayor of Vienna. During the two previous years the emperor, Franz Joseph, had succeeded four times in preventing his instalment, in spite of popular support. But it was only a postponement.

B'nai B'rith arose in answer to this turning point in Austrian politics, to the need to confront antisemitism and to redefine its identity in the face of the failure of emancipation and of the ideals of tolerance that had been the basis of the *Bildung*. The years during which Freud was a member of B'nai B'rith were those in which the echo of the 'Dreyfus Affair' was still strong, when France had been torn and divided, the France of Zola's *J'accuse*. Zola was the *non-Jew* with whom 'one can reach an understanding'. Those were the years when Jewish socialist and democratic organizations flourished in the area of forced residence in the Tsarist empire, the years of Zionism and Bundist autonomism. B'nai B'rith was part of this process of affirming dignity that had been offended and humiliated, which Freud joined under the impulse of new and traumatic events in his life, among which one of the most important was his father's death in 1896.

In the first years after he joined, Freud was particularly active in the association. He not only gave lectures but was a member of the juridical commission and head of the cultural commission. He was part of the staff in charge of searching for new members for the creation of a second 'lodge', the *'Eintracht'* [Harmony], with which he put close friends and colleagues in touch: Oscar Rie, the family paediatrician; Eduard Hitschmann, one of the most faithful pupils and an assiduous attender of the Wednesday meetings, who was later to be in charge of the first psychoanalytic clinic in Vienna; and, finally, his friend Königstein, who, with Theodor Herzl, the founder of the Zionist movement, was to have an important place in the series of Roman dreams with reference to antisemitism and the struggle for emancipation.

Freud's younger brother, Alexander, joined B'nai B'rith in 1901. He was to be one of the intermediaries for contacts with the association in later years, when growing involvement in the psychoanalytical movement and then his illness would force Freud to reduce the number of social activities he engaged in within the association.

It is not going too far to say that in those early years B'nai B'rith functioned as 'an intellectual forum' (D. B. Klein), where

Freud corroborated his ideas by expounding them to a wider audience that acted as a resonance box and supported him with their enthusiasm. At B'nai B'rith, Freud gave a total of 21 lectures, a third of them in the years between 1900 and 1902, during the period immediately preceding the creation of the Viennese Psychoanalytical Society. After this entirely Jewish phase, the psychoanalytical movement acquired its first non-Jewish followers. Jung and Binswanger joined in March 1907, and Ernest Jones the following year. Freud's fear that psychoanalysis would remain an exclusively 'Jewish national affair' was vanquished, although this alone would not be enough to protect the psychoanalytical movement and the new science from the ferocious attacks of latter-day inquisitors, with their delirious ideas of 'Aryan', 'Christian', and 'anti-Jewish' psychology.

The first lecture given by Freud at the B'nai B'rith was on 7 December 1897 and was on the subject of dreams. The amount of enthusiasm to which this gave rise was so great that he talked on the subject again to the same audience a week later. At the end of the second talk Freud told his audience of the 'intelligibility and the meaning of dreams'. On the same occasion he also announced his intention of writing a book about dreams. This third lecture was on the subject of 'The Psychology of Forgetting'. Six months later Freud published 'The Psychical Mechanism of Forgetfulness' (1898b). In the following year he gave a lecture on the psychical life of children. This was followed by a lecture on the mechanisms of superstition, which was later to be developed in *The Psychopathology of Everyday Life* (1901b), and by another lecture on dreams.

In the two lectures on Zola, Freud discussed his ideas about the French naturalist writer in some depth. In particular, the second lecture was given to commemorate the writer's death. In the remaining lectures Freud introduced discussions of the objectives of the B'nai B'rith Jewish movement and the role of women in the organization.

In 1904 the work of Moebius and the code of Hammurabi were discussed. This was the occasion on which Freud introduced his early views about Moses. He then went on to talk about the physiology of the unconscious, the role of psychology in civil administration, jokes, the psychological function of baptism, and the character of Hamlet. In the talk 'What Is Psychoanalysis', in November 1913, Freud offered a theoretical definition of the divergences that were by then separating him from Carl Gustav Jung. Some of the concepts developed here were taken up again in two important contributions in the following year. The last three lectures were devoted, respectively, to the theme of death, to the work of Anatole France, another writer who was highly considered on account of his commitment to fighting against antisemitism, and, finally, to the role of phantasy in artistic creation. When he gave his last lecture, Freud was already 61 years old. His fame had spread to America some time before that.

The lecture reproduced here is the only one whose original text has been preserved. The subjects dealt with were to be taken up again in 'Thoughts for the Times on War and Death', published in two parts in the same year in *Imago* and later included in the complete works under the same title (Freud, 1915b). This is a rare occasion for us to find in Freud's writings examples of concordance and variations between two texts written for different situations. In some circumstances Freud preserved, or sent to his closer colleagues, notes that he later reviewed. Some examples are the 1934 unpublished notes on *Moses and Monotheism*, discovered by P. C. Bori (1979, pp. 331-335), the notes on the 'Rat Man', and the imaginative outline of the 1915 twelfth metapsychological essay, discovered in Ferenczi's papers (Freud, 1915b). However, this is the only known case where two versions of the same work have been kept; both of these versions were thought through, developed, and printed for two different purposes. In the first the audience are 'the Brethren' of the Jewish association, with which Freud speaks warmly, avoiding any technicalities, whereas in the second the audience is one of specialists and colleagues, with whom he communicates in a written form. In the transition from the lecture to the essay printed in *Imago* there is evidence of greater precision in style and concepts and semantic sliding; passages touching on the Jewish monotheism have been expunged (see also the Translator's Introduction). Also expunged are the humorous Jewish jokes that Freud used to capture his audience: the one about the Jewish mother who turns to the Rabbi when her son has an accident, or the one about age ('the Jew is always aged between 60 and 120 years')—particularly significant for a man who himself was aged 59.

Those that have been kept have been divested of any specific reference to Jewishness. The reference to 'we Jews' is replaced by a more generic *we* in which we can all recognize ourselves. In particular, two significant observations about Jewish religious life have been expunged: the 'refusal' of the idea of 'original sin' and the highly positive evaluation of earthly life as against the illusions of the afterlife. These, according to Freud, were some of the causes preventing Judaism from asserting itself 'with the decadence of ancient religions' as a 'world religion'. To these two ideas Freud was to add a third in the three essays on *Moses and Monotheism* (Freud, 1939a [1937–39]): the purity of monotheism and the rejection of idolatry. These aspects of Jewish religion contributed, according to Freud, to giving a unique impulse to the development of intellectual representative activity. But they were also the cause of a *loss* of contact with more archaic psychic activity. Also expunged are the *patriotic tones* in relation to the victorious German soldiers that seemed to inebriate him at first. The first months of the war put to the test his feelings and anglophilia. (See Freud's correspondence during these years with his brother, who was anti-British, and with Ernest Jones—cf. P. Gay, 1988.)

The image of Judaism felt by Freud was substantially taken up by the *Wissenschaft*: Judaism as a religion purified of any reference to myth. (See L. Baeck, 1905, 'Das Wesen des Judentum'. Baeck was rabbi of the Reformed Jewish Community in Berlin from 1912 until his deportation to the concentration camp at Theresienstadt in 1943. It is worth noting that in the same year as the publication of Leo Baeck's work, the most 'beloved' of Freud's pupils, Otto Rank—whose real name was Rosenfeld—wrote an essay under the same title, in which he explained the Jewish presence in the disciplines of psychology and psychoanalysis in terms of a specific vocation—D. B. Klein, 1981, pp. 132–137.) This was a view that Freud substantially shared, without, however, being prepared to follow through the whole apologetics of the matter. 'Moses the Egyptian' and the paradoxical significance he gave to a religion that became 'fixated' at the father stage and therefore, from the point of view of religious evolution, was reduced to an extent to a fossil was the price Freud *paid* in return for unparalleled exaltation of the ethics and the moral and intellectual heights reached by Judaism by virtue of those 'fixations'. This reminds us of the pages of the celebrated essay on the *Witz* (Freud, 1905c), pointing out the awareness that the most successful Jewish jokes have of the deep connection existing between the defects of Jewish life the joke is criticizing and its great 'qualities'. Judaism, according to Freud, in its stronghold of humanitarian representation, was in danger of not being adequately aware of the degree of rejection it was undergoing by a society affected with a veritable psychosis of anti-Jewishness. This is one of the hidden meanings of the observations about the 'obscure memories of mankind' which Judaism 'has carefully kept apart', disqualifying itself therefore from being a 'world religion'. Historically speaking, psychoanalysis is an attempt to go beyond this dilemma by elaborating the conflict that has been introduced into the superego as a result of assuming a 'higher' degree of morality. In this light, the problem of 'civilized' man coincides with that of Judaism. Both are paying for the introjection of aggressive drives with the burden of imaginary guilt and are showing themselves to be incapable of facing up to aggression from other people. From this point of view, psychoanalysis could be said to be connecting itself with those sources and to be taking on the task of retrieving the lost secret through removal of the destructive drives. This is where we meet the *other scene* of the universal ethical appeal, 'Where id was, there shall ego be'.

These pages are a testimony to the strength of Freud's Jewishness in his reflections on the destiny of mankind and society, and its role in the very repositioning of his scientific discoveries, of the place they held in the dialectic of culture and civilization. In these pages we can glimpse the meaning attributed to the feeling of belonging by a sector of western Judaism of which Freud was an exponent; and for new forms of expression for an autonomous and independent Jewish existence, and the creation of a universal science.

During the first few months of the war, Freud was openly pro-German. But this attitude was short-lived and in any case had to be understood in the context of the general opposition from Jews at that time to the antisemitism of the Russians. Serving his country on the eastern front, wrote his son Martin on his way to fight in the war, was 'the best occasion to express my frank aversion to Russia'. As a soldier he enjoyed the exclusive satisfaction of being able to cross the Russian frontier without the special permit imposed on all other Jews by the restrictive laws of the empire (see Gay, 1988). The first military operation was awaited in the climate of warfaring excitement of the time—like 'a thrilling mountain climb' (8 August 1914, in Gay, 1988). The idea that it would be a short conflict was still strong. With Lou Salomé, a Russian of aristocratic origin who had a brother fighting alongside the 'white troops', his tone stayed at the level of morality required in a 'republic of letters' to whose principles Freud tried to remain faithful, even during those months: 'I do not doubt that mankind will survive this war too, but I know for certain that neither I nor my contemporaries will ever see a trouble-free world again. It is too ugly' (Freud to Lou Salomé, 25 November 1914, in Pfeiffer, 1972). When he wrote 'Mourning and Melancholia' (1917e [1915]) and 'On Transience' (1916a), he found the words he needed to express his position publicly and to maintain the degree of morality required of a true man of science and learning. The fall of the Tsarist regime and the Balfour declaration, which he greeted with 'enthusiasm' (letter to Abraham, 10 December 1917, Freud, 1907–26) gave him a glimpse of something positive in the general catastrophe the people of Europe were living in, when he himself was forced to act personally to help his family suffering from the scarcity of food. 'A German victory', he was to write to Jones soon after the war, would have resulted in a much harder blow to the interest of mankind (letter to Jones, 15 January 1919, in Gay, 1988). Gratitude to the statesman whose name is associated with the plan for a 'Jewish foyer' led him to send Balfour an extract of his 'Autobiography' to thank him for the 'honorary support' given by Balfour on the occasion of the inauguration of the Hebrew University in Jerusalem (9 June 1925, in Gay, 1988).

In leaving a systematic treatment of Judaism for a more appropriate occasion, Freud not only gained in precision but brought out in the clearest way possible what was in danger of being lost by the confusion and superimposition of a specific form of self-representation of Judaism belonging to a particular period and generation of Judaism, as opposed to the whole array of forms in which Jewish consciousness had expressed itself historically.

The pages about the destruction of the precious heritage common to all mankind that had been brought about by the psychosis of war bring out clearly his identification with an outlook on life that belonged to a whole generation of Jews. Freud lost no opportunity to point out that trust in progress and civilization had been the result of an illusion right from the start. There was no need to wait for war to notice the presumed morality of 'these great nations', who could be supposed 'to have acquired so much comprehension of what they had in common, and so much tolerance for their differences, that "foreigners" and "enemy" could no longer be merged, as they still were in classical antiquity, into a single concept' (Freud, 1915b, p. 277). Observation showed, to be sure—added Freud significantly—'that embedded in this civilized state there were remnants of certain other peoples, which were universally unpopular and had therefore been only reluctantly, and even so not fully, admitted to participation in the common work of civilization, for which they had shown themselves suitable enough' (Freud, 1915b, p. 276).

> Relying on this unity among the civilized peoples, countries, men and women have exchanged their native home for a foreign one, and made their existence dependent on the intercommunications between friendly nations. Moreover anyone who was not by stress of circumstances confined to one spot could create for himself out of all the advantages and attractions of those civilized countries a new and wider fatherland, in which he could move about without hindrance or suspicion. In this way he enjoyed the

blue sea and the grey; the beauty of snow-covered mountains and of green meadow lands; the magic of northern forests and the splendour of southern vegetation; the mood evoked by landscapes that recall great historical events, and the silence of untouched nature . . . [a] new fatherland [that could be] a museum for him . . . [where] as he wandered from one gallery to another . . . he could recognize with impartial appreciation what varied types of perfection of mixture of blood, the course of history, and the special quality of their mother-earth had produced among his compatriots in this wider sense.

And with reference to the immortal classics, he added (Freud, [1915b]):

none of these great men had seemed to him a foreigner because they spoke another language . . . and he never reproached himself on that account for being a renegade towards his own nation and his beloved mother-tongue. [pp. 277–278]

Nor did Freud even refrain from speaking in the *first person* in the conclusion, asking himself rhetorically for what mysterious reason

the collective individuals should in fact despise, hate and detest one another—every nation against every other—and even in time of peace. I cannot tell why that is so. It is just as though when it becomes a question of a number of people, not to say millions, all individual moral acquisitions are obliterated, and only the most primitive, the oldest, the crudest mental attitudes are left. [p. 288]

The rejection of the crowd, which in Freud's case was almost a phobia, had its roots in an ancient memory borne out by experience that where crowds are gathered and shout—even when those crowds are demonstrating for progress—there is always a danger of a *pogrom*. The connection of these pages with Freud's feeling of his Jewishness becomes evident if they are compared with what he was later to write about the role of the Church and the army—two institutions Jews remain outside *par excellence*

(Freud, 1921c)—and if one compares them with the acute observations about the narcissism of minor differences and with the criticism he levelled at the foundations and the consequences of evangelical morality. (In the same light, see the criticism of the Soviet system—cf. Freud, 1930a, pp. 114–115.)

In 'On Transience' (1916a) Freud wrote that war destroyed not only 'the beauty of the countrysides through which it passed and the works of art which it met with on its paths', but (Freud, 1916a):

> it also shattered our pride in the achievements of our civilization, our admiration for many philosophers and artists, and our hopes for a final triumph over the differences between nations and races. It tarnished the lofty impartiality of our science, it revealed our instincts in all their nakedness and let loose the evil spirit within us which we thought had been tarnished for ever by centuries of continuous education by the noblest minds. It made our country small again and made the rest of the world far remote. It robbed us of very much that we had loved, and showed us how ephemeral were many things that we had regarded as changeless. We cannot be surprised that our libido, thus bereft of so many of its objects, has clung with all the greater intensity to what is left to us. . . . [p. 307]

These were words in which, through a memory of a discussion he had had in the summer of 1913 with the poet Rilke, Freud transferred the grief he still felt for the break with Jung into his feelings of loss at the destruction of the war. (Freud's article opens with a reference to a discussion that had taken place two years earlier, 'with a taciturn friend and of a young but already famous poet'—probably Rainer Maria Rilke—during a holiday in the Dolomites (ibid., p. 305). 'What remains of the [psychoanalytical] movement,' he was to write to Jones in December 1914, 'after Jung and Adler, is now succumbing to the struggle between nations' (see Gay, 1988). In the form in which they are expressed, these words were to sound even truer after the rise of Nazism. The world would become small for those who sought to flee from the grip of Hitler's advance, and men's hearts would appear terribly far away and remote when the British coastal batteries, for fear of reinforcing the convergence of political interests between the Axis power and Arab nationalism, put an end to the last hopes of those who had fled from the Nazi inferno, had been rejected by all other countries, and had then sought refuge on the shores of their native land. The connection between these pages of Freud's and the problem of Judaism becomes clear if they are compared with what he was to write two decades later, in reference to the influence of Moses on the formation of those characteristics that Freud considered as pertaining to Judaism (letter to E. Freud, 1938, in E. Freud, 1960): that it is a characteristic of real Jews to renounce nothing and to seek recompense for what has been lost. The model for this, in Freud's judgement, we have in Moses, who has made a lasting impression on the Jewish character.

The suffering of the saddest losses throughout life, together with frequent changes of land and language, is here assumed as a parameter of an ethical imperative not to succumb to despair. Although it is really 'sad to have to judge even world events from a Jewish point of view,' one cannot 'do otherwise' (letter to A. Zweig, 16 October 1935, in E. Freud, 1970), without running the risk of perpetuating the illusion that everything was as before. The pages written 23 years earlier in order clinically to understand the psychical mechanism of melancholia can be adapted to describe the drama involving Judaism at the time. Like the person suffering from melancholia, the 'non-authentic' Jew who makes a show of belonging where he is not in fact recognized and idealizes a culture that rejects him, or, worse, copies pan-German nationalism and shows himself to be 'more German than the Germans', is in reality a man who has been rendered incapable by tremendous fear and anguish at the thought of looking at the world realistically, at acknowledging the most terrible of all losses and accepting for this the mourning and depression that follow from it.

Freud wrote in 1915 (1917e [1915]):

Mourning is regularly the reaction to the loss of a loved person, or to the loss of some abstraction which has taken the place of one, such as one's country, liberty, and ideal.

> ... In what, now, does the work which mourning performs consist? I do not think there is anything far-fetched in presenting it in the following way. Reality-testing has shown that the loved object no longer exists, and it proceeds to demand that all libido shall be withdrawn from its attachments to that object.

But

> this demand arouses understandable opposition—it is a matter of general observation that people never willingly abandon a libidinal position, not even, indeed, when a substitute is already beckoning to them. This opposition can be so intense that a turning away from reality takes place and a clinging to the object through the medium of a hallucinatory wishful psychosis. [pp. 243–244]

At the basis of '*Jewish Selbsthass*', as of any other form of cultural self-deprecation induced by persecution, there is a situation where right from the start identification with the majority culture is the result of *a seductive misunderstanding*, which makes highly explosive the ambivalence that is inevitably produced when processes of integration, interaction, and assimilation between the majority and the minority come into place. This seductive misunderstanding becomes explosive when external rejection on account of his radical differences condemns the person seeking integration to reject totally his very origins, or to take on his position as a fringe member of society as a positive role. This, as has already been pointed out, was the situation that Freud recognized as being that of German-speaking Judaism, directly establishing a connection in the very choice of terminology with the eminent genealogy of Spinoza and Heine. The 'authentic Jew', when the gravest of losses has been recognized as such and when he has got over his mourning, should in this light start, *like Moses*, to look for a suitable substitute.

> *Le bruit est pou le fat,*
> *Le plainte est pour le sot;*
> *L'honnete homme trompe,*
> *S'en va et ne dit mot.*

[A fuss becomes the Fop,
A fool's complaints are heard;
A gentleman betrayed,
Depart without a word.]

[From *La Coquette Corrigé*, a comedy by Jean Sauve' de la Noue (1701–1761), quoted by Freud (1938c), p. 301.]

PART ONE

JUDAISM AND PSYCHOANALYSIS

CHAPTER TWO

A cultural event within Judaism

David Meghnagi

The problem of links and connections in Freud's work with the original Jewish cultural hinterland of the founder of psychoanalysis is dealt with in this chapter with reference to the long-term cultural history. The birth of psychoanalysis is considered here as a cultural event within Judaism and as a sublimated answer to the problems posed by secularization and the rejection of an authentic integration of Jews into Christian–European society. In the words of Kafka, psychoanalysis is a comment by Rashi on the present generation of Judaism, on its joy and suffering. In these pages Freud's work itself appears as a metaphor for the long historical journey of

---

This chapter reformulates and synthesizes the hypotheses expressed in 'Freud e la coscienza ebraica contemporanea', in: AA.VV, *Ebrei moderni* (pp. 96–112), edited by D. Bidussa (Turin: Bollati Boringhieri); 'Freud e l'immaginazione ebraica', in: *Modelli freudiani della critica e teoria psicoanalitica* (pp. 89–100) (Rome: Bulzoni, 1985); and 'Freud', in: AA.VV., *Studi freudiani* (pp. 85–96), edited by D. Meghnagi (Milan: Guerini Editore, 1989).

Judaism from a place of 'non-existence', which, however, offers its members warmth and the certainty of belonging, to a wider and more living reality, where the ego expands and also exposes itself to the danger of becoming lost in a world without sense. The exploration of the 'mystery' of how the Jews preserved themselves as a people and why they attracted 'such inextinguishable hatred' is looked at again here in the light of a powerful need for re-appropriation of identity, which for Freud was never lost but was still operating and should be positively revindicated in order to face up to the necessities of the moment. From this point of view Freud's work and his reflections on Judaism might be better understood with reference to the other analogous attempts to find answers to the dilemmas of contemporary Jewish life, from Rozenzweig to Kafka, from Schoenberg to Buber and Einstein.

[ED.]

Freud's writings, like those of many other great exponents of contemporary culture, would not have been possible without the edicts of emancipation following the French Revolution. It was in fact during the revolution that the ghettos, which had for centuries enclosed the Jews all over Christendom, finally opened up. Historically speaking, the rise of the psychoanalytic movement is part of a vast movement, involving contemporary Judaism in the face of the great problems that had to be confronted when the ghettos were opened up and later, during the antisemitic and racist reactions. It may be a coincidence, but the discovery of the 'Oedipus complex' on Freud's part coincides with two other great moments in contemporary Jewish history: the first congress of the Zionist movement in Basel and the rise of the Bund, the first socialist organization in the empire of the Czars. The Zionist movement was founded by another Viennese Jew, Theodor H. Herzl, who had been horrified at the feelings unleashed by the Dreyfus affair. We know from his correspondence with Fliess how much such dramatic events were experienced by Freud on a personal level, to the point that they were introduced into the *Traumdeutung* itself, with the dream of the 'Roman Gate in Siena' and the reference to Psalm 137 and the 'exiles of Babylon'. The Bund, on the other hand, arose in the East, in the area from which Freud's forebears came and where towards the end of the last century the concentration of Jews was greatest. The Bund, as opposed to the Zionists, called for cultural and national autonomy, 'the right to dignity' in the lands inhabited by Jews for centuries. Zionists and Bundists were therefore in contrast with each other, but they were both, albeit from different positions, in conflict with the dominant forces of the time, and they saw in the movement for democracy and socialism and the abstract idea of equality the answer to the problems of the Jews (Meghnagi, 1985b).

Psychoanalysis arose in the midst of these conflicts, which involved Jewish society both in the East and in the West, and was itself one of the answers. In his own way, Kafka had understood this when he stated in December 1922, in a letter to Werfel (which was probably never sent), that psychoanalysis 'is the comment of Rashi on the present generation of Jews', on their 'joys and sufferings'. As a measure against facile enthusiasm, Kafka invited people to bear in mind the historical complexity out of which the Freudian discoveries had arisen, and the fact that they were a 'metaphor' for a state of obstruction in history. Kafka did not accept Freud's theories, but he could not avoid being aware of the importance of the great state of ferment within Jewish society in the West which went under the name of psychoanalysis. The 'father complex', which psychoanalysis universalized, was really, in Kafka's opinion, the problem of the relationship between the emancipated Jewish son and his Jewish father, of a state of belonging that was therefore sometimes refused but never really overcome, and of the accusation of a double state of belonging, in which the Jews who had come out of the ghettos could see themselves, even when they believed they had severed all contact with their origins.

Kafka thus intended to combat the risk of banalizing the dramatic situation in which the Jews of his time found themselves involved, the danger of their blaming themselves, of concealing the real significance of the problems the generation of emancipated Jews was experiencing, of fleeing from their historical responsibilities. Obviously this is not the case with Freud, who never failed to admit this sense of responsibility and who, thanks to a sort of deliberate rather than forced self-isolation, was able to entertain a unique and exemplary relationship with Jewishness, as distinct from the great literary production that goes under the name of 'German–Jewish symbiosis' or central European culture.

In this respect it is interesting to compare the solutions both men found for a problem that was of historical as well as existential significance. Both Freud and Kafka were aware that their writings were a place for sublimation of the anxieties of a whole generation. Both aspired to the universal, in the sense that their problem, in order to rise to the dignity of 'scripture', had to find solutions that were valid in all places—in Freud's case, by means of a proposal that was at once theoretical and scientific; in Kafka's, through recourse to a literary model in which the historical problem is transposed to a cosmic cycle that is cryptic and, one might add, gnostic and kabbalistic.

Kafka eliminated all references to his Jewishness in his stories and relegated instead to his diaries and letters all clarification of hidden meanings in his writings. Freud, on the contrary, who defended to the last the scientific character of his discoveries and who was at first terrified in case his work might degenerate into 'a Jewish national affair', seemed, instead, almost to be doing everything he could to create doubt in his readers that things might be otherwise, or at least more complex than he gave to understand. (In order to overcome resistance from the Viennese group to the choice of Jung as the first chairman of the International Psychoanalytic Association, Freud reminded them of the danger that psychoanalysis might fall victim to antisemitism (cf. the letter to Karl Abraham on 3 May 1908—Freud, 1907–26—and those following of the same period; for a general evaluation, cf. Gay, 1988).

It seems paradoxical that psychoanalytical knowledge, as opposed to other forms of knowledge, cannot fail to preserve, as it proceeds, 'substantial traces of the motivational processes that oriented its creator' (see chapter six, this volume). In other words, psychoanalysis becomes science and breaks through into a field that is strictly literary, whereas great literature, on the other hand, is so only because it conceals those traces and so reveals more. In Kafka, literature and Jewishness coincide, and the loss of a sense of roots, even though these may be wandering roots, becomes unhappy literary wandering. (On this aspect of Kafka's writing, cf. Meghnagi, 1988, pp. 18–20.)

What Freud explains with reference to universal structures operating in all people in all places appears in Kafka as a human problem, common to all people, in *an extreme situation* prefigured by him in *The Trial*. The theme of nakedness, analysed by Freud (1900a, p. 243) with reference to the 'Naked King' in Andersen's fairy-tale, has a parallel in Kafka's *Trial*, where K's condition means he has not even a name to refer to in the face of a Power that has become totally extraneous and incomprehensible. As Hannah Arendt (1966) has pointed out, Kafka puts K in the condition that society expected of Jews so that the assimilation could work in a non-traumatic way: a condition of absolute isolation and a loss of one's very sense of existence.

The analogy could be extended by tracing the historical origins of the nakedness theme, that is, by going back to the early models elaborated in Spain during the Inquisition. While bearing in mind the obvious differences in the historical situation, the comparison cannot fail to strike home. In both cases escape through conversion appeared as an illusory solution that did not cancel the stigma of an origin felt to cause indelible guilt and to be a source of permanent insecurity. In both cases the hunt for the 'hidden Jew' resulted in raving accusations of secret plots and in the exalting of an ideal of 'racial purity'. In both cases the victim found himself deprived of the very moral bases for resistance to the culture that excluded him.

In order to survive, the converts elaborated a secret religion that was increasingly further removed from the original but which showed obvious traces that could not escape the Inquisition's vigilant and paranoid eye. The emancipated Jews, on the other hand, even when they themselves thought they were extraneous to the world of their ancestors, which they could even openly oppose, nevertheless preserved traces of it that did not escape the notice of modern-day inquisitors. It would be interesting to ascertain how indebted to their Jewish origins such authors as Saint Teresa of Avila, Montaigne, and perhaps even Cervantes himself were. (On the 'Naked King'—The Tale of the King's New Clothes—cf. Castagnoli Manghi & Terracini, 1982, pp. 187–236; on Teresa of Avila and Miguel Cervantes, cf. Sara Rossi, 1983, 1987.)

The modernity characterizing these and other writers, the fact that they lend themselves to interpretations that can explain the drama of modern man, depends largely on a similarity of problems—the fact that they never belonged entirely to the society they were part of, even when they were acknowledged and accepted by it. Although he did so with the hatefulness of defence which rings more bitter than attack, the young Marx took up an anti-Jewish code that was then prevalent and with which he identified, and he used it to make an appeal for the juridical emancipation of Jews, in the manner of a brilliant Talmudist student who is able to reverse the very terms of a problem and create new possibilities of thought. In a similar way, a writer so deeply marked by *Selbsthass* as Simone Weil can continue to produce treasures that are the result of her rejected origins and so open up Christian scriptures to a new way of seeing the world. There is an underground link that has not yet been completely explored connecting the great outbreak of creativity from the second generation of Jews in the nineteenth century—those who were emerging from the ghettos of Europe—with a new *'forma mentis'* that had slowly formed over the centuries thanks to the privileged relationship Judaism has always had with literature and which was based on the Book, the place in which to project anxieties and phantasies, in a search for answers and for different questions. Anyone with even elementary knowledge of the world of 'Midrash' knows how much the particular technique that goes under the name of 'free association' has for centuries been one of the traits of the traditional Jewish method of reading and commenting on the Scriptures. In 'Midrash Haggadah' any clue, any similarity of sound in different words, a new meaning produced by different words that are found together, or by a subdivision into several smaller words, the numerical value of a group of words, and so on, is enough to discover other meanings that might have been hidden. Certain Talmudic comments, to say nothing of the bold speculations of the mystics, which Jews have practised with for centuries, almost equal the boldest speculations that psychoanalysis has prepared us to accept. What Freud ingeniously did was to introduce this technique, or rather certain aspects of it, into the very heart of the psychological and psychiatric knowledge of his time, thus causing an implosion (Meghnagi, 1989b).

On a cultural level, Freud's work is a product of that great process of secularization of culture sweeping through the Jewish world from the beginning of the seventeenth century onwards, whose great exponent in the Sephardic Diaspora (the emigration of Jews from Spain during the Reconquista and the Inquisition) was Baruch Spinoza. Between the Zfat mystics' speculations and Freud's discoveries there lie three decisive centuries for the birth of a new Jewish *'forma mentis'*. These are the years of conversions and heresies that upset Jewish society from within, of the outbreaks of Sabbatianism, of the visionary plans of Molko and Reubeni and the more concrete and sensible plans of the Duke of Naxos, who succeeded in repopulating Jews in the regions of Upper Galilee. These were centuries of profound change in Jewish life, which prepared the way culturally for the adoption of more secular attitudes and entry into the world of modern thinking. From Spinoza to Freud, from the Kabbalist mystics to Kafka, there is a long, secret chain in which the historical phases are marked by the emancipation edicts and the great 'clash encounter' the Jews emerging from the ghetto would have with the prevailing trends of European culture to which they opened themselves up as no other group did at the time, almost to the point of 'losing themselves' in a new universal synthesis. The emphasis Freud gave to his position of 'conquistador' (letter to Fliess of 1 February 1900; see Masson, 1985) in the field of science cannot be explained merely by his proud revindication against the rejection he came up against initially.

It is part of a situation that unifies into the same symbolic register his being a Jew and the new science he was struggling to create. In the same way as Jewishness seemed to defy all codification, so psychoanalysis appeared in comparison with the stronger sciences to be lacking in object, something undefinable and unsettling; suspended in a permanent limbo and dependent on codes elaborated by the other sciences and never on its own, in order to justify itself.

I have mentioned the link between the work of Freud and that of Kafka. There is also a third writer who should not be forgotten: Walter Benjamin. As has been pointed out by Scholem, the great scholar of Jewish mysticism, the choice made by these three writers was to put themselves positively on the fringe and then to use their fringe position as a declared vantage point in order to look into the depths of history and the psyche. What characterizes Freud, as it does also Benjamin and Kafka, is the constant awareness of what one really is: writing in German without being a German, and refusing any form of camouflage.

On a wider plane, one might also relate Freud's attitude to that of another great founder of the 'German–Jewish synthesis': the poet Heinrich Heine, whom Freud admired. Heine was writing at a time when the sirens of the *Bildung* could still sound genuine, but he was never dazzled by them, nor taken in. Fully conscious of his special condition, he did nothing to conceal it, either from himself or others. Even though he had to give in and, like others, undergo conversion in order to obtain, as he himself was to say, 'the passport to enter the society of his time', Heine maintained his sense of distance, which saved him from the danger of becoming a *'parvenu'*. His personal tragedy then became the source of his inspiration. For a time, Heine was attacked and later obliterated by the Nazis because of this ability of his to see through and show up the hidden nature of certain underground currents in German society. One need only mention the explosive and provocative text in which are evoked the demoniacal powers that could spread over Europe once Germany had taken on its true aspect and rid itself of its Kantian mask and its great philosophy, substituting the god Thor. Heine spoke to the century of enlightenment so that it should not be caught unawares on the day when this would happen. The situation in which Freud would find himself is at the end of the cycle described by Heine. He began writing when the *Bildung* ideal had begun to fade and Germany was about to show the face of the god Thor, and this was why he openly defended 'that something' which was 'so precious' that 'made him feel Jewish', and was so insistent on doing so (1925d [1924], pp. 7–9, note 1; Freud, 1925e [1924], p. 222; 1941e [1926], pp. 273–274).

Certain pages of the brief and densely written 'Das Unheimliche' (Freud, 1919h) seem almost to have sprung from Freud's mind to give an explanation for the logic of antisemitism and the sinister feeling of anguish and paralysis of many German Jews about an event that was so familiar to them but which they deluded themselves into thinking belonged to the past.

In order to defend themselves, Jews who had grown up among the ideals of the *Bildung* were forced to 'reconquer' their Jewishness—that which they might have rejected and considered as belonging to the past. They had to go back to being what, in spite of themselves, they continued to be accused of being secretly!—to the place they had believed, or deluded themselves, they had left through baptism and change of name. The sense of loss was a double one, since going back meant also acknowledging that they had always lived an illusion, that prejudice had never really been overcome, and that their rejected, or lost, identity had in fact become the only means of survival—acknowledging, therefore, that the choice was not between 'being a citizen like any other' and persisting in the status of a 'person from the ghetto', because in fact there was no choice; and if they wanted to resolve the illusion, they had to acknowledge their fate of being 'pariahs' (Arendt, 1958). It may also be for this reason that Faust's famous maxim, *'Was du ererbt von deinen Vätern hast, Erwirb es, um es zu besitzen'* [what you have inherited from your ancestors, acquire it yourself, in order to possess it], was among those that Freud was most fond of, and it appears three times in his writings in reference to problems pertaining, at least indirectly, to the question of Jewishness: first in *Totem and Taboo* (1912–13, p. 158), with reference to the transmission of certain 'psychic predispositions' between generations; then in the introductory lectures (1916–17, p. 355); and, finally, and significantly, at the end of the section 'The internal world' in *An Outline of Psycho-Analysis* (1940a [1938], p. 207).

The same observations can be made about Freud's writings on civilization (Freud, 1930a). The problems described here, with reference to the human race, appear again in the three essays on Moses, as a historical problem of Jewishness. In effect, as I have tried to show elsewhere, Freud's entire scientific thinking is bound up with his reflections on the state of Jewishness (Meghnagi, 1987a). And his great strength lies in the fact that this thinking gave rise to a universal theory of human actions. In their own way, the racists had understood him, and hence this was one of the reasons for their banning of his work.

In Freud, Jewish creativeness met with the great trends of enlightenment and positivism, the language they used and their meticulous experimental research, and was able to look beyond the Jewish condition of despair to the condition of all people everywhere. Chased back into the realm of the 'demoniacal' and rejected by culture, Jews 'went back' to being theorists of the unconscious with Freud. In Freud, the 'father's Jewishness'—which, as we have seen, obsessed a fair section of western Jewish intelligentsia—was transformed, without, however, being rejected as a historical problem, into the general problem of the relationship with one's father and the law. An object of primitive passions that deny existence to other people, the Jew 'came back' into culture as a theory of transference. Rejected and isolated with the raving accusation of 'deicide', the Jew 'took his revenge' with a theory that makes the murderous instinct towards the father, and the consequent feeling of guilt, the very basis of ethics. Considered in this perspective, the entire edifice of psychoanalysis could appear retrospectively as a great Jewish joke, the most successful joke by a Jew against the culture of his time. The accusations made against the Jews were shown up and at the same time validated in their character of delirium: society hates in the Jew what it rejects in itself; fundamentally, hatred of Jews is 'hatred of oneself' projected onto the Jews. Brought back to its character of a construct of fantasy, the Freudian myth was an answer to the Jewish 'hatred of oneself' and to the introjection of the antisemite stereotype common to many of the emancipated Jews themselves. With his work Freud provided the world of emancipated

Jewish intelligentsia with a new frame of thought within which to situate and give meaning to the feeling of isolation and rejection that society caused in return for their entering it and being genuinely integrated: a way of avoiding the sense of despair and a means of re-founding one's identity and the identity of other people. The Jewish group functioned as a 'specialized subgroup', to use Bion's terminology. The edifice of the psychoanalytic institution retraced the internationalism of the Jewish communities, providing a model of identity that replaced that of religious ideology or the patriotism of modern political states.

Scholem, the great historian of Jewish mysticism, liked to include among the great 'sects' of contemporary Judaism the circle that formed around the Warburg Library and the Institute for Social Research, known as the 'Frankfurt School'. This metaphor of Scholem's, which is not exactly congenial to those in question, could also be applied to the association created by Freud, which, until Jung joined it, was almost exclusively composed of Jews. There is no doubt that the message of the three groups aspired to the universal; it is also true that within them there were also those who declared they were extraneous to the Jewish tradition. Nevertheless, this rejection did not exclude their belonging, and on a wider historical plane this type of Jewish existence, known as 'German–Jewish symbiosis' and 'Central European literature', has indeed been one of the forms of western Jewish existence, a way in which one section of contemporary Judaism experienced its Jewishness. To insist on ignoring the links with Jewish life would be to repeat on other levels the mistake of the doctor of science who refuses to accept the truths of psychoanalysis.

The attitude of democratic culture towards racial madness has in many ways been comparable to that of the positivist doctor towards Schreber's paranoia: 'the Jews do not exist, they are merely the work of antisemites'. And if there were millions of people in the East with their own language, history, and culture, this referred at most to other people, not 'our Jews' in the West. A close reading of western publications about Jews from the end of last century up until the rise of Nazism, and also in the early post-war years, would reveal the same short-sightedness.

It must be said that Freud was always very clear about this, and the painful, soul-searching meditation of the three essays on Moses is ample evidence, beyond the limits characterizing it for its 'Lamarckianism'. Freud brought into the patient's descriptions, in the dialogue between analyst and patient, all that seemed irremediably suffocated and blocked up in society. Enclosed in a room, the 'dialogue' between Jews and non-Jews could be taken up again and continued as an analysis of the resistance that is produced in any dialogue, of ancestral fears that cause the differences between human beings to be arbitrarily increased so as to escape the anguish of a lack of identity. In reference to this kind of problem, Freud writes in *Civilization and its Discontents* (1930a, p. 114) of 'narcissism of minor differences'.

For Freud, the truth is always elsewhere: in the most radically banished of the patient's words, in his apparently meaningless symptoms, in a *lapsus*, it is possible to trace a piece of truth that is asking to be explained. If anything is left over, one must always turn around and begin again, as in Isaiah's great metaphor. In Freudian strategy the loss of a sense of origin, the assimilation that European Jews seek in emancipation, is not a cancellation of one's existence. For Freud there is always a trace through which to go back to something archaic, which he jealously preserves and considers to be operative even in the present. At certain times what he says seems almost to be 'in collusion' with the antisemites, who preached a demoniacal Jewish entity secretly plotting against Christian and European civilization. In reality, between the two registers there is the same distance that separates Schreber's delirium from Freud's discoveries about the mechanisms of paranoia. Between the two registers is the gulf that separates fact from psychosis and perversity. Unlike what happens in all-inclusive romantic reductiveness, in Freud's reasoning multiform reality is never levelled down to an undifferentiated simplicity: Jews as a single category, as a symbolic abstraction quite different from actual existence. At the same time Freud perceives the limit of a culture, that of democracy and socialism, which has difficulty in understanding how the problem regarded a dialectics of symbols and not only the actual life of individuals.

It is curious how this aspect of Freud's work has remained partially obscured with respect to a more 'genuine' or 'universal' Freud. Those who thought they were censuring these aspects were not only committing an act of self-censure and psychic denial, but were striking at the heart of one of the most significant characteristics of psychoanalytic elaboration, that of being closely linked with the profound experience of an entire generation. The traces disseminated everywhere by Freud in his writings are not of secondary importance. On the plane of strictly psychoanalytic research they function as 'constructs' for a new science, a science that is autonomous and universally valid.

On the cultural plane they reveal what Jewishness had become for Freud and how Jewish self-perception continued to survive and to be transmitted from generation to generation, in spite of the apparent loss of a sense of origin. Unless one wants to go back to superseded notions of what makes a culture what it is, one has to admit that this has been one of the ways in which Jewish consciousness has reflected itself in its very historical evolution. As Freud himself is led to acknowledge in the last page of *Moses*, if he cannot exhaust the subject of Jewishness (and, one might add, of Christianity), at least he is able to tell us how it functioned in his mind as a producer of new forms of knowledge.

On the historical plane the choices Freud made were emblematic and sense-giving for all those Jewish thinkers of the time who, excluded from the possibility of acting directly on the course of events, made research their aim in every field of knowledge: from Einstein in physics to Schoenberg in dodecaphonic music, from the study of society in the grand, exacting work of an Alsatian rabbi's son Emile Durkheim to the powerful research of the Frankfurt School, to Cassirer's investigations of the myth, and to those of Popper about the very bases of scientific knowledge, to the admirable work of encyclopaedic collecting by Aby Warburg, another rabbi's son, born in Hamburg 'with a Florentine spirit and Jewish blood', of a library of 60,000 volumes—a personal re-edition of the ancient Talmudic cult of the Book and a unique project of its kind. Apart from the feeling and perception regarding their Jewish origins shared by these and other writers of a unique period, a hidden link flows through them all, independently of the awareness they may have had of it. As Hannah Arendt (1966) has rightly pointed out, they started from an unresolved knot in their historical condition to elaborate a grand new idea of humanity that was valid for everyone.

PART TWO

HISTORICAL ASPECTS

CHAPTER THREE

Some thoughts on Freud's attitude during the Nazi period

Janine Chasseguet-Smirgel

Since the Second World War, it has become almost normal to associate antisemitism with right-wing and reactionary movements. But during the course of the nineteenth century this was in no way a foregone conclusion. There was, instead, an unceasing struggle that went on within the workers' movement itself. Babel's famous slogan that 'antisemitism is socialism for imbeciles' was more than just a motto. It shows just how difficult it was in the democratic and socialist movement itself to fight against the germ of a hatred whose roots lay in remote and almost impregnable corners of the psyche and fed on ancient fears that the great social changes helped to render explosive. However paradoxical it may seem today, the antisemites' hatred of the emancipated Jews who are not recognizable by any distinctive marks and mingle with the rest of the popula-

---

First published in the *Revue Internationale d'Histoire de la Psychanalyse 1*: 13–31 (Paris: Presses Universitaires de France, 1988). Reprinted by permission.

tion, 'contaminating' it with the possession of its women and 'secretly plotting' against it, could be far greater than hostility towards traditional Jews, who at least 'could keep in their place' and at night slept inside the walls of their ghettos. It is no coincidence, moreover, that hatred of modernity and everything connected with it has been historically related to hatred of that part of the population that derived the very conditions for entry into society from the birth of modern concepts. The fact that Judaism itself paid for this entry with an unparalleled upheaval did not alter this attitude much. The Jews remained the principal object of all reactionary feelings in that they were the tangible image of the change that had taken place with the collapse of the old feudal order, the very negative image of modernity, the symbol and quintessence of capitalism and democracy, of socialism and communism.

So in order to justify the need to fight against antisemitism, it was for a long time necessary to demonstrate, if not that the Jews themselves had proletarians in their midst, then at least that this struggle was necessary from the proletarians' point of view, which was not always easy since there were also those who justified antisemitic agitation as the first stage of an 'anticapitalist' awareness. Becoming clearly aware that antisemitism was an evil in itself, the most odious and aberrant manifestation of hatred between human beings, was no easy thing to do. In order for people's thinking to change it took several decades and, above all, the greatest catastrophe in modern European history—the rise of Nazism, the war, and the extermination of the Jews.

Mention of these aspects is essential in order to understand not only Freud's Jewishness but also the conception he himself had of it: Judaism as the religion of reason in contrast to the irrationalistic utopias pervading the culture of his time, especially in Germany. This idea of Judaism is common to a whole generation of emancipated Jews. As Mosse has rightly pointed out, the historical origins go back to the brief, prolific period of the *Bildung*, with which Freud identified. His liking for Goethe went in the same direction, and one could argue that the prize he received in 1930 was a sort of 'acknowledgement on the part of the Jews', since there were so many Jews present in the 'Goethe Associations'.

What distinguishes Freud from other representatives of German Jewishness is not the shared ideal of the *Bildung*, but the way in which he shared it, transforming everything that Germanic society rejected in Jews into open, positive revindication. Freud's position was the specific one of a person taking up a stance of positively understood marginality within a tradition. Like Kafka, whose thinking was encouraged by the outlying position of the place he lived in with regard to the great centres of German culture, Freud transformed into something positive what to many German Jews had seemed to be a stigma to be rid of or to hide from.

Among the criticisms levelled at Freud there is one that is particularly malicious: that he sacrificed the necessity for an open battle with dictatorial regimes, and with Nazism in particular, to the survival of the movement he had founded. In its most malicious form, this criticism centres on the fact that some of his followers (non-Jews), in order to continue working, agreed to collaborate and compromise themselves with the Nazi regime. In this orgy of accusation nothing has been spared—not even the subtle irony of the phrases he asked to be added to the declaration he was forced to sign before leaving Vienna for exile in London ('I would advise anyone to experience the Gestapo!').

To involve the victims in the responsibility for the persecutions they have suffered—states Chasseguet-Smirgel—is one of the ways of perpetrating persecution and the culture of indifference in other forms. Apart from the fact that the responsibility for compromising themselves with the Nazis lay with the non-Jewish analysts who did so, the criticisms levelled at Freud are shown to be devoid of foundation as soon as one analyses what Freud wrote and did during his lifetime, especially if one bears in mind the context in which he found himself living and working. The first part of Chasseguet-Smirgel's work deals with the reconstruction of this historical context. In a long historical digression the author shows the seriousness of the climate of antisemitism in the German-speaking area (and not only there) long before the Nazis came to power, and how such a climate not only contributed to rendering the Jews more and more isolated, but also disarmed them completely by forcing them to 'hate themselves' and 'reject themselves'. All this makes all the more significant the fact that Freud was left untouched by this syndrome and at all times retained the awareness of the distance separating him from the rest of German society, and that through his work he indicated that the rejection of themselves by many of the German Jews was the gravest of the dangers facing Jewish people.

[ED.]

Unhappily, the material needed to describe and understand Freud's attitude during the Nazi period is sadly lacking. Consequently, one has to reconstruct. I start with the hypothesis that it is impossible to understand Freud's attitude and to form an opinion about it without first going back into the past and placing the issues at hand into their historical and ideological contexts. Secondly, I attempt to assemble certain elements on the basis of which I believe it is possible to reach some kind of a conclusion regarding Freud's sentiments and his attitude towards Nazism. A historian would have done more justice to this section than I. Its psychological implications are such, however, that I cannot pass the subject over in silence.

Jewish assimilation from the days of the Enlightenment onward and in Freud's time

Generally speaking, there is ample material in his works demonstrating Freud's fidelity to his Jewish heritage. Yet one can point to other passages seemingly indicating an unconscious desire to deny his Jewishness. In my opinion, *this alloy of opposing elements is an intrinsic part of Jewish identity.* When analysing Jewish patients, one should aim at making this a conscious contradiction, not at resolving it. For two thousand years, being a Jew in the Diaspora has meant accepting one's place in the long line of those who silently pick up their hats out of the gutter where a Christian has thrown them. This can never go without conflict. The best way of bearing such a situation and the lowering of self-esteem that accompanies it, at least until the Enlightenment, was to adhere strictly to the Jewish religion, which teaches its followers that they belong to a chosen people—a small Bedouin tribe at the outset—to whom God has entrusted the Law and who are to become His priests. It was this notion of having been elected that enabled the Jewish people to accept the enormous instinctual sacrifice and the intellectual, even aesthetic, asceticism that went with the renunciation of paganism and idolatry. It is through religion that the Jewish people are able to retrieve their dignity, and the Bible, as Heinrich Heine has so beautifully put it, becomes their 'portable homeland'. Heine—a Jew who converted because, as he has said in a well-known phrase, 'To become baptised is to hold the ticket giving access to European culture'—perfectly expresses this self-esteem sustained by religion in one of his 'Hebrew Melodies', called 'Princess Sabbath', from which I quote an extract:

Princess Sabbath

In the book of the Arabian Nights
We see enchanted princes
Who sometimes take on
Their ancient shape and beauty.

My song glorifies a Prince
whose destiny is such, Israel
his name. And the formula of a spell
Has changed him into a dog.

A dog with the thoughts of a dog
He acts the scruffy outcast the whole week out
In the mud and the filth of life
Scoffed at by the kids of the street.

But each Friday, at evening time
As it turns to dusk, suddenly
The spell breaks and the dog
Becomes a man once more.

A man with human feelings
A head held high, a lofty heart in his breast
In feast day clothes, as is befitting
He enters his Father's house.

The Enlightenment will have a twofold effect on the destiny of European Jews. On the one hand it will considerably weaken religious faith, including Judaism; on the other, it will, to a greater or lesser degree, associate the Jews in its humanitarian and humanistic upsurge. Enlightened non-Jews, such as Lessing, will plead in favour of Jewish emancipation. Moïse Mendelssohn, Lessing's protégé, writes: 'Fortune is in our favour since it is impossible to insist on human rights without calling for our rights at the same time' (quoted by Hanna Arendt, 1958). During this period there was no Jewish liberation movement to help Jews maintain their identity. The choice was between becoming 'a man of the Enlightenment' or remaining in the ghetto. There was a growing impatience, and Jews began to seek 'to change the Jew's place in the state' (David Friedländer, quoted by Hanna Arendt, 1958). Thus in 1799, in his *Epistle to Some Jewish Heads of Family*, David Friedländer states that he is in favour of baptism as 'an open demonstration of integration into society'. Religious leaders were far from welcoming the idea, but the movement to become converted had taken root and was to continue, even during the Napoleonic occupation, when full citizenship was granted to the Jews of several German states, these rights being rescinded upon Napoleon's downfall (see Sachar, 1958). In most German states it was impossible, as a Jew, to have access to culture. The universities, in particular, were closed to Jews, as were a great number of the professions.

In her book on *Rahel Varnhagen* (1958), Hanna Arendt describes the antisemitism and self-hatred of this Berlin Jewess, who gathered the personalities of the romantic literary movement around her in one of the best-known salons of the day. She wrote to her brother, for example:

The Jew within us, it is this we must exterminate, be it at the cost of our lives. This is a sacred truth.

The Jews are a divided, torn and tattered nation, and what is worse, they are the object of a well-deserved scorn.

Successively, every possible course must be tried: changing one's name is of 'decisive importance'; this makes her 'on the outside, into another person', so she believes at least. The next step is to become baptised; . . . 'there is no reason why one should want to hold on to a semblance of the religion of one's birth. . . . And most important of all: 'to have one's children baptised. They must never hear us speaking about these follies of history in any way other than we would speak about the rest of history.'

This near-melancholic assault on the ego containing her Jewishness did, however, cease shortly before she died. At the very end of her life Rahel Varnhagen began to write again in the characters of the Hebrew alphabet and, according to her husband, said on her deathbed: 'To have been born Jewish has been for so long in my life the ultimate shame, my most bitter and painful burden. Henceforth it is something I would not renounce at any price.'

The reason I have briefly described the itinerary of this German Jewess in the first 30 years of the nineteenth century (she died in 1833) is that the picture it gives of Jewish assimilation as it then was and as it was to continue for at least another century is typical, even though somewhat of a caricature. It goes hand in hand—and this can never be overemphasized—with the entry of Jews into European economy and culture. Assimilation does not always take on the antisemitic character and the refusal to accept one's self we see in *Rahel*. In other cases it can be a distressingly painful wrench that will be bound up with a pathetic resistance. Heine, for example, said he was simply 'baptised, not converted', and swore to 'ardently take up the Jewish cause and to fight for equality of civil rights; in the harder times that ineluctably lie ahead of us, the Germanic scum will hear my voice. It will ring out loud enough to be heard in the beer gardens and palaces of Germany' (quoted by Hanna Arendt, 1958).

Yet the Jewish problem will be solved neither by conversion nor by assimilation. At the beginning of the century, in a brochure published in Prussia under the title 'Against Jews', Grottenauer announces that he is not referring to 'any Jews in particular, not to any one Jew, but to Jews in general, the Jew as he is everywhere and nowhere' (quoted by Hanna Arendt, 1958) and states that in his opinion the Jews who are seemingly merged into the population are more typically Jewish than Jews in their robes—words that prefigure modern antisemitism.

One can, in fact, venture that antisemitism—the doctrine of racial prejudice—developed as a relay to anti-Judaism—opposition to the Jewish religion—*because of the very success of Jewish assimilation*. It is significant that the term 'antisemitism' was used for the first time in 1873, though granted during a period of economic crisis, by the German journalist Wilhelm Marr (quoted by A. L. Sachar, 1964), whereas the constitutional law founding the German Empire and which accorded Jews the same rights as all other German citizens was dated 1871 (Rürup, 1975).

Closer to Freud's day, in 1844, that is, twelve years before he was born, we have Karl Marx's article 'On the Jewish Problem', written in reply to the theses of Bruno Bauer. Karl Marx, the grandson of a rabbi and son of a converted Jew, is representative of the destiny of Jews descended from the Enlightenment. [To cut short on any objections to the effect that considering Marx as a representative of the Jewish *Selbsthass* is to demonstrate one's ignorance of Marxism, and that establishing a relation between Marx's words of hate with regard to Judaism and the modern antisemitic madness is to commit an error of judgement, let me state that (1) history forbids any absolute caesura between theories that manifestly follow one from the other: opposition to Judaism cannot be separated either in theory or chronologically from modern antisemitism; and (2) where vocabulary is the same, the concepts expressed can hardly be fundamentally different.]

I feel justified therefore in quoting a few of Marx's pronouncements, following straight from the assimilationist position, the natural consequence of which is *Selbsthass:*

What is the secular foundation on which Judaism is built? *Practical needs, personal interests.*

> What is the Jew's secular cult?
> *Trafficking.*
> What is his secular God?
> . . . *Money.*
> . . .
> What is the Jewish religion really based on?
> *Practical need, egoism.* This is why, in reality, Jewish monotheism is nothing more than a polytheism of multiple needs, a polytheism which of its own accord sets up latrines as an object of divine law.
> . . .
> Money is the god of Israel before whom no other god has the right to subsist.
> . . .
> The god of the Jews has become secularized, transformed into a worldly god. The true god of the Jews is the bill of exchange.
>
> The law obeyed by the Jews, which is neither founded nor deeply rooted, is but a religious caricature of a moral code that is neither founded nor deeply rooted. . . . [italics in original]

For anyone inclined to believe that Judaism only comes under attack as another of the many religious alienations (and even so, where the Jewish problem is concerned, nothing one says, even in the middle of the nineteenth century, can ever be entirely innocent), let me quote the following passage:

> Christianism is sublime intelligence of Judaism, Judaism is the vulgar application of Christianism . . .

These were two German-speaking Jews. Otto Weininger, author of the book *Geschlecht und Character* [*Sex and Character*] published in 1903, is a third, quoted by Freud in a note in 'Little Hans'. In addition, Weininger was mixed up in some murky affair between Freud and Fliess. His work was commented upon in Central Europe for many decades. Weininger was Freud's contemporary, and, what is more, he came from Vienna. He committed suicide the year his book was published. One chapter in this book marked by pathological misogyny is called 'The Jews'. Let me quote a few extracts:

> The *Jew's* vicious antisemitism proves that no one knowing him well finds him loveable....
>
> Jews, like women, prefer movable property to real-estate. ... This is the explanation for Jewish fascination with communism. ... [The Jew utterly ignores] the very notion of a state. ... This is why all Zionist endeavours are bound to fail.
>
> The Aryan longs to learn about his ancestors ... he honours them because he attaches a value to the past, which is not the case with Jews. [sic]
>
> [Jewish life] can be compared to the rhizome which spreads across the entire earth.
>
> The Jew must give up the impossible undertaking of seeking to respect himself for being a *Jew* in the way the Aryan does, and concentrate instead on making it possible to consider him as a *human being*.
>
> ... the divine in man is none other than his soul, *which the absolute Jew is without*. There can be no more outrageous an insult to the God of Christians than to identify Him with the God of the Jews. This is not a religion born of pure reason, but the superstition of an old woman and a vile fear.
>
> The fact of escaping into the material, the need to bring everything back to material issues, suppose the absence of an intelligible ego and are therefore essentially Jewish characteristics. [italics in original]

As for Jehovah, he is 'an *abstract idol* before which he [the Jew] is filled with a *slavish terror* [Weininger's italics]. In short: 'the Jew is truly "God's accursed child on earth."' [Although several of Weininger's phrases seem to echo those of Marx, others are more in the vein of Hegel.]

This *Selbsthass* is not confined to the nineteenth century. It will continue into the twentieth century, as can be seen in much of Simone Weil's work, to choose but one of many other authors. We find her launching into attacks against the Jews that are completely in line with the preceding examples. Here, for instance, is a passage taken from 'La pesanteur et la grâce' (quoted by Giniewski in his book, *Simone Weil ou la haine de soi*, 1978):

Israel, everything is sullied and appalling, as if so purposed, from and including Abraham onwards (with the exception of a few prophets). As if to very plainly warn: Pay heed, here is evil!

A people chosen to be blind, chosen to be Christ's executioner. The Jews, a handful of wanderers without roots, have caused the uprooting of the whole terrestrial globe. . . . The curse of Israel weighs on Christianity. The atrocities, the Inquisition, the extermination of heretics and unbelievers, this was Israel. Capitalism is Israel (and still is to some extent). . . . Totalitarianism is Israel, especially in its worst enemies.

In an unpublished text (examined by Giniewski), Simone Weil expresses her wish 'to see Jewish parents encouraged not to tell their children that they are Jewish' (p. 47).

My aim, with the help of these four examples, is to show the context within which Freud's Jewish identity developed. For many this is common knowledge. Others—Jews and non-Jews alike—will find these facts astonishing and label them as a psychosis. We must never forget that this Jewish psychosis was a part of Freud's environment. And for all its unpleasantness, there must be no mistaking *the cause* of it: namely, antisemitism.

This brings me to the situation in which Jews found themselves at the turn of the century and between the two World Wars. Antisemitism was virulent at the time, and attempts to find solutions can schematically be divided into first three and then four categories:

1. The religious solution: that is, constant inner and outer struggle to maintain Jewish faith and law, accompanied by segregation, which was not only imposed from without but also, up to a certain point, sought by those concerned, this being inevitably related to the assertion of Jewish identity. Jews who had become part of the surrounding society and cultural environment were rejected.
2. Assimilation: a solution that ranged from discarding certain religious practices to total denial of Judaism and, taken to its extreme, meant, as Rahel Varnhagen had advocated before, raising children who knew nothing of their Jewish

origins—even bringing them up to be antisemitic, a 'solution' adopted frequently for the offspring of mixed marriages.
3. The Zionist solution: this started to emerge around 1870 and took shape with the publication of Theodor Herzl's book *The Jewish State* (1896), the direct consequence of the Dreyfus case.
4. Finally, at the end of the nineteenth and the beginning of the twentieth centuries, Jewish intellectuals and proletarians massively rallied to communism. As we know, the Bolsheviks refused autonomy to the 'Bund' movement they created. The solution to the Jewish problem which communism was to procure and in which so many Jews placed their hopes—guided in this by a socialist ideal stemming directly from the Bible, though they were often unaware of this—led to the most total crushing of Jewish identity ever, as demonstrated by the absolute refusal of the Soviet regime to recognize the specific nature of the 'final solution', considered as a mishap of capitalism, the execution of Jewish poets and writers by Stalin, the affair of the 'white-coat assassins' conspiracy', the systematic non-recognition of Jewish culture, the present-day anti-Zionist propaganda, which day by day maintains that the concentration camps came into existence as a result of Nazi and Zionist collaboration, and so on. But I shall say no more on this particular aspect of the question, since we have no evidence to prove that Freud was ever, even if only momentarily, attracted to communism.

To be a Jew of the Diaspora, living in the conditions that reigned at the end of the nineteenth and the first third of the twentieth century, and not to experience ambivalent feelings with regard to Judaism would be purely and simply to escape the laws governing the human psyche.

As for those who reproach Freud with showing traces of ambivalence towards his Jewish identity, I fear they are mistaking the effects for the causes. Had there not been antisemitism, this ambivalence would certainly have been lessened. Those who accuse the Jews of that time with not perfectly identifying themselves with Judaism are siding with the choppers-off of arms who treat their victims as 'dirty amputees'. Additionally, all in all, Freud was a 'good Jew'.

It must not be forgotten that on the collective level assimilation led to the religious reform, which, in its extreme form, is nothing less than a group madness of sorts. In certain cases German rabbis recommended abandoning the fundamental symbols of Judaism such as circumcision, celebration of the Sabbath on Saturday (in certain reformed synagogues in Germany this was celebrated on Sunday), and Hebrew, for which German was substituted. Lastly, only the religious aspect of Judaism was asserted, to the detriment of its nationalistic characteristics (Samuel Holdheim [1806–1860] and Abraham Geiger [1830–1874]; the latter published a prayer-book expunged of all prayers that expressed the wish to restore a Jewish state in Palestine and to rebuild the Temple—cf. Epstein, 1959).

There can be no judging of Freud's attitude until one has allowed for this individual and collective madness generated by the antisemitism of the environment. This madness is, I believe, the prelude to the *Gleichschaltung*, the bringing-to-heel, the forced levelling, of all German institutions by the National Socialist Party, and the dissolution of whatever was not '*volkish*', a 'final solution' of a mild nature insofar as Jews disappeared from the point of view of their identity but did not, as yet, physically disappear.

Freud faced with his Germanic background and Nazism

At the age of 17 Freud joined a nationalist student group, and during the First World War his sympathies were wholeheartedly on the German side. Jones quotes Freud as saying: 'All my libido is given to Austria-Hungary' (Jones, 1953–57, Vol. 2, p. 192). Here it is worth noting that Freud more often than not claimed that he was 'German' (not Austrian). His letters to Abraham show him rejoicing in Germany's victories and concerned with its defeats. On 15 January 1919, however, he writes to Jones: '. . . that a German victory might have proved a harder blow to the interests of mankind in general' (Jones, 1953–57, Vol. 2, p. 321).

Freud received a classical education, which gave him an international cultural background. This contributed to the universalization of psychoanalysis. German writers to whom he refers are those in the humanistic tradition, Goethe being the best example. This does not prevent the unavowed influence of German romanticism from creeping into his work, as Henri and Madeleine Vermorel have shown in 'Was Freud a Romantic?' (1986) and which I attempted to interpret in 'The Paradox of the Freudian Method' (Chasseguet-Smirgel, 1985). Likewise, the Jewish side of Freud's culture goes far deeper than is visible in his writings when its often unconscious aspects are taken into consideration. For instance, a relation is to be established between the central role accorded the Oedipus complex, the *Vater complex*, and Jewish monotheism.

Facts hinting at the attitude Freud adopted with regard to his Germanic background during the Nazi period are essentially to be found in his correspondence with Arnold Zweig (E. Freud, 1970). Here, in counterpoint, assertions of his Judaism and Zionist sympathies stand out very plainly. On 7 January 1932, Freud writes:

> *Dear A.Z. My wife thinks that the photograph of an old Jew sent you at Christmas cannot have reached you. I am just writing to ask whether I should send you a replacement. Ever yours*
>
> *Freud*

On 8 May 1932, he writes to 'Meister Arnold' in Palestine, where the latter had emigrated:

> *... how strange this tragically mad land you have visited must have seemed to you. Just think, this strip of our mother earth is connected with no other progress. ... Palestine has never produced anything but religions, sacred frenzies, presumptuous attempts to overcome the outer world of appearance by means of the inner world of wishful thinking. And we hail from there (though one of us considers himself a German as well; the other does not); our forebears lived there for perhaps half or perhaps a whole millennium. ...* [emphasis added]

On 17 June 1936, he jokingly rebukes Meister Arnold:

My Jofie is a stickler for accuracy and does not like being called Zofie by you; Jo as in Jew.

He is referring to his chow-chow. 'Jofie' is Hebrew for 'pretty'. In other words, less than a year before Hitler came to power, Freud affirms he is a Jew, only a Jew, a Hebrew descendant, an attitude he maintains for the rest of his life. His motherland is Palestine, meaning that he simultaneously renounces all ties to the German people, because he is the one to consider that he is not (or is no longer) a German. In fact, on 18 August 1932 he again writes:

So perhaps the Nazis are playing into my hands for once. When you tell me about your thoughts, I can relieve you of the illusion that one has to be a German. Should we not leave this God-forsaken nation to themselves?

Those wondering why Freud remained silent as the dark clouds of night gathered over Europe should remember that in 1933 Freud was 77 years old and had been suffering from a cancer for ten years. On 25 October 1933, he writes in his letter to Meister Arnold:

I am fit to work once again but I cannot climb my stairs, am therefore under house arrest. I think this time I have established my right to sudden fatal heart attack, not a bad prospect. . . . I am hardly likely to write anything again. . . . It reminds me of that Chasen [Hebrew for the precentor in the synagogue] *of whom it was said: he'll live, but he won't sing.*

And on 28 January 1934: '*I am not working any more: my organs don't cooperate properly.*' On reading through the letters he wrote to his close friends during this period, one can detect the pain he was suffering, not to mention his discreet, and in most cases humorous, references to the jaw operations he underwent and his prosthesis. Jones notes in his account for the year 1934 that the Freud family rented a house in Grinzing, adding: 'part of the garden, being steep, was only accessible to him in a bath-chair' (Jones, 1953–57, Vol. 3, p. 202).

But over and above age and sickness, what weighed most heavily on Freud—and those who accuse him today pay little heed to this—was quite simply the situation in which the Jews of Europe found themselves throughout the Nazi period. How can anyone with even a slight knowledge of history imagine that Freud could have publicly protested against the Nazis and the fate reserved for Jews in Europe without worsening things for Jews in general, and more especially for analysts? This amounts to totally ignoring the current madness of the day, a madness that was again present, in essence, in 1986 in the disputes centring around the study of the German 'historian', Emil Nolte, who defends the thesis that since Haim Weizman, future President of the State of Israel, had proclaimed that the Jews were going to join with the English to fight against Germans, Hitler's only course was to declare war in 1939 and to track down and exterminate the Jews. In addition, according to the same historian, Hitler did nothing more than borrow the idea of concentration camps from Soviet Russia. He just copied the 'Asian solution'—here one is to understand Jewish solution—since the pioneer communists were, for the most part, Jews (a discussion in *Die Zeit*, Series 29–49, October–November 1986, between E. Nolte and J. Habermas, E. Jäckel, H. Schulze, M. Broszat, and T. Nipperdey).

Even though today there are sufficient numbers of people in the world, and in Germany, who do not think along these lines and who criticize such ways of thinking, this was not the case in the 1930s, when every word uttered by a Jew was snatched up and ground to powder to extract the only thing that counted: the final product—that is, a magma—from which cause and effect had disappeared, meaning the disappearance of logic based on the paternal principle (as Bela Grünberger has said, *the father is the cause of the child*). This is the *Gleichschaltung* applied to productions of the mind. All protests by Jews become the *cause* (and not the effect) of antisemitism (an ahistorical mode of thinking, which I have described in 'The Archaix Matrix of the Oedipus Complex', 1984), in the way the assassination on 7 November 1938 of Vom Rath, counsellor of the German Embassy in France, by the Jew Grynspan—an act of despair and protest against Nazi exactions—became the pretext for the *Kristallnacht* (9–10 November 1938), the night that windows of Jewish shops and synagogues were smashed, some synagogues were burnt, and Jewish shops were looted.

During these years Freud's thoughts were, in fact, constantly turned to the Jewish problem. [In my opinion, the key enabling us to understand *Moses and Monotheism* (1939a [1937–39]) in its entirety is missing; the work does, however, contain a question Freud asked himself: 'Why Jews?' (see his letter to Arnold Zweig, 30 September 1934, in E. Freud, 1970). I refer anyone wishing to go into this issue in greater detail to Ostow's (1982) book, *Judaism and Psychoanalysis*, particularly Martin Bergman's excellent article 'Moses and the Evolution of Freud's Jewish Identity'. Nevertheless, I consider that we have not yet discovered all the intentionalities of Freud's *Moses*.] On 8 April 1933, just two months after Hitler came to power, Freud wrote to Marie Bonaparte (in Jones 1953–57, Vol. 3, p. 188), '*I am glad, and it makes me proud to hear, how much sympathy and help you are showing the victims of the persecution in Germany*'—but he is convinced that if the Nazi movement spreads to Austria '*it cannot lead to such excesses*'. This optimism was shared by 90% of European Jews. To foresee the horror that lay ahead of them would have meant nothing less than identifying with the Nazis, which, for various reasons connected, amongst others, to the conditions the Jews had borne for centuries and the accusations projected onto them, proved impossible. Here again, this is an effect of antisemitism and one that even Freud did not escape. On several occasions he expressed the hope that '*we in Austria should be spared the German ignominy*'. (letter to the Spanish poet Xavier Boveda, 6 December 1933, in Jones, 1953–57, Vol. 3, p. 196). On 13 February 1935, however, in a letter to Arnold Zweig, he writes: '*I see a cloud of disaster passing over the world, even over my own little world.*'

On 2 May 1935, he again writes: '*My idea of enjoying spring on Mt. Carmel with you was, of course, only a fantasy*'; then he goes on to tell Zweig about the short address he had written for Thomas Mann's sixtieth birthday: '*I have slipped in an admonition which I hope will not pass unnoticed.*' In fact, after the First World War Thomas Mann had adopted a nationalist stand that did not augur well, and Freud's admonition was worded as follows (1935c, p. 255):

> *I can allow myself something else, however. In the name of a countless number of your contemporaries I can express to you our confidence that you will never do or say—for an*

> author's words are deeds—anything that is cowardly or base. Even in times and circumstances that perplex the judgement you will take the right path and point it out to others.
>
> Yours very sincerely
>
> Freud

His message was heard, we know—for in fact *the only people having the possibility to speak out against Nazism and antisemitism were non-Jews*. According to Jeanne Lampl-de-Groot's communication to the Hamburg Congress of the API in July 1985, Felix Boehm had sought Freud's opinion about German analysts faced with the obligation imposed on them by the Nazis to exclude Jewish analysts from the D.P.G. 'I have nothing to ask of them, nor do I require anything of them', Freud responded, in the only way possible (with dignity, aloofness, and somewhat bitterly). Those in the habit of giving lessons—Germans and others—who insist that Freud should have responded otherwise either do not understand or have forgotten what Nazism was and the situation of Jews in Europe. In addition, as I have remarked elsewhere (Chasseguet-Smirgel, 1986), they are unconsciously taking part in the Nazi enterprise of rendering Jews responsible for the fate that met them. What happened to the Jews in the twentieth century is the problem of the Christian society in which the Jews lived, a society which, in addition, was, as of the nineteenth century, infiltrated in Germany by a return to paganism. As I see it, the often violent accusations that are levelled against Freud today are to be considered as a return of the repressed. The problem lies in the silence of the Aryans, not in the silence of Jews. The attitude that consists of heaping blame onto the victims is a highly suspicious one in my opinion. Is this not the best way of clearing oneself of the guilt of this genocide that lies on the shoulders of us all?

On many occasions (especially in *The Ego Ideal*, 1973) I have stressed the importance of the *Hilflosigkeit* [helplessness] of the new-born infant, a concept Freud describes in *Inhibitions, Symptoms and Anxiety* (1926d [1925]) in particular. The following passage is well known:

> The biological factor is the long period of time during which the young of the human species first finds itself. Its intra-

uterine existence seems to be short in comparison with that of most animals, and it is sent into the world in a less finished state. As a result, the influence of the real external world upon it is intensified and an early differentiation between the ego and the id is promoted. Moreover, the dangers of the external world have a greater importance for it, so that the value of the object which can alone protect it against them and take the place of its former intra-uterine life is enormously enhanced. The biological factor, then, establishes the earliest situations of danger and creates the need to be loved which will accompany the child through the rest of its life. [pp. 154–155]

In the same text, Freud also states:

... just as the mother originally satisfied all the needs of the foetus through the apparatus of her own body, so now, after its birth, she continues to do so.... What happens is that the child's biological situation as a foetus is replaced for it by a psychical object-relation to its mother. [p. 138]

The situation of Jews in Europe during the Nazi period was such that they were reduced to the *state of helplessness of the new-born infant*, and the succession of losses they experienced placed them once more in man's original state of defencelessness. This was not solely a matter of losing their rights, first in Germany, then in Austria, and then in occupied Europe (the Nuremberg Laws), nor was it, as yet, a question of their physical annihilation, as a result of which six million perished. It was the permanent accusations to which they were subjected by the Nazi propaganda and fascist literature of Europe, and the impossibility of escaping these accusations, since all previous attempts at assimilation had failed and their 'defect' supposedly ran in their very blood. Now *all accusations*, however outrageous or contradictory, *meet with an unconscious truth*: we are all grasping, cruel, greedy, and ambitious. These accusations led to feelings of dereliction, linked to an *abandonment by the superego*. In addition, every member of society joined in the chorus, or, at best, said nothing. In other words, the friends, neighbours, and 'allies'—in short, all our fellow creatures who in part act as a substitute for the lost matrix that provided nourishment and protection—were strangely absent. And lastly, a good internal object cannot be maintained in a relentlessly hostile environment without it being endangered to some degree. It is never totally acquired, and the ups and downs of life reinforce it or cause it to disappear, establishing in its stead a cruelly exacting agency that plunges the subject into a dark abyss.

Faced with 'the happenings within the international psychoanalytical society' and the fact that 'Austria seems bent on becoming National Socialist', Freud wrote to A. Zweig on 22 June 1936 (in E. Freud, 1970):

> *Fate seems to be conspiring with that gang. With ever less regret do I wait for the curtain to fall for me.*

And until the final moment, when, on 23 September 1939, the curtain fell for him, Freud remained a faithful Jew and—*to the best of his ability*—maintained fidelity to his Jewish identity, as can be seen from the correspondence that is accessible to us.

Rendering Freud responsible for the fact that German analysts joined the institutions of the Third Reich is, it seems to me, derisory and absurd. I would even go as far as saying that this is yet another way of continuing the persecution. Freud was only one more Jew standing before the machine the Nazis had set up to eliminate Jews psychically and physically. He was nothing or 'Nobody's Rose', to quote the title of a collection of Paul Celan's poems (1963) in which the poet reproaches God with not having been there at the Shoah. But God's desertion is none other than man's desertion, and His silence is the silence of us all.

PART THREE

CULTURAL ASPECTS

CHAPTER FOUR

The Jew as an ethical figure

Silvia Vegetti Finzi

In this contribution the author proposes to show how some aspects of Jewish life, which were at the basis of psychoanalysis, have ended up by assuming an importance that goes beyond the specificity of Jewishness, becoming exploitable and recognizable by a wider symbolic world. But the entry of Jews in their own right into western culture, the fact that for many people their history has taken on the character of a general parable, does not prevent them from affirming their specificity, 'even though an affirmation' of their 'diversity' may in some contexts have become 'more difficult' and 'almost impalpable'. Acknowledging the fruitfulness of psychoanalysis as something rooted in a decentralized minority culture increases its power to criticize and emancipate and causes it to make a critical evaluation of its own institutionalization, which is inevitable in any case. Allowing a cultural experience and a historical tradition to interact enables us to make up 'culturally' for a 'historically' imposed fringe position, for a 'non-belongingness' decreed in the name of genetics but interpreted in terms of criticism and a refusal of what exists. From this point of view, the Jew becomes 'an ethical figure', 'a collector of tension', and an interpreter of unease, a bridge between the past of *'arche'* and the future of *'telos'*.

[ED.]

Psychoanalysis grew up, towards the end of the last century, in the context of Viennese Jewish culture and remained limited to this sort of society until Freud's meeting with Jung in 1906. Only three years later, Jung became Chairman of the International Psychoanalytical Association and Editor of the *Jahrbuch*, and accompanied Freud on his lecture tour of the United States.

From that moment onwards psychoanalysis left the confines of the Jewish minority and gradually became (apart from interruptions due to the two world wars) the *koine* of western culture that it is. In spite of being adapted to different national registers, to different schools of thought, to theoretical and technical re-elaborations, to misunderstandings, and to the systematic resistance to it that has grown up, one element has prevailed over and above the therapeutic practice: the internalization of conflict.

In this sense psychoanalysis has exported not only the urbanistically and culturally closed nature of the ghetto, but the Jewish experience of life itself.

On a close look, the emancipated Jewish community anticipated some of the characteristics of modern and late-modern society. The decline of the traditional agricultural economy and the types of feudalism connected with it favoured those who, like the Jews, had a form of culture that was not linked to inheritance and private income. In most European countries, Jews were prevented from owning land and holding public office. On the other hand they were, to a certain extent, allowed to conduct commercial and financial activities and later to enter the professions, such as medicine and law. One of the greatest historians of Jewish society, Leon Poliakov, has claimed that with the arrival of technological civilization the world became Jewified. According to him, our civilization has become Jewish in the antisemitic sense of the term. If we consider the cultural characteristics of technological society, we can identify a series of attributes that are typical of the Jewish minorities: the separation from agrarian society, intense territorial mobility, a decided tendency to urbanism, adaptability to transformations, a competitive spirit, an open-minded attitude towards money-making, and the internationalizing of economic and commercial relationships.

Identification of Jewishness with modern society is so great that criticism of capitalism and modernization has often taken the form of antisemitism. Even the Jewish Karl Marx wrote in *Das Kapital* that capitalists were 'intimately circumcised Jews'. However, apart from the convergence of Jewishness and modernization in the broad sense, I should like to draw attention to a characteristic of late-modern society we are experiencing now.

At the present moment relationships of communication are prevailing (at least in terms of self-representation) over those of production. The exchange of information seems to be becoming more important than the exchange of goods. In this context, the dominant anthropological figure is in many respects similar to that of the emancipated Jew. Their experience in the world of commerce and banking had, from very early on, refined Jews' communicative skills, both in the sense of extending language ability (see the example of Canetti's autobiography) and in the sense of the relating of different cultures. Life in basically insecure social contexts had perfected not only relationship skills but also means of self-control and the ability to tolerate frustration.

One need only think of the episode that Jacob Freud recounted to his little son about being assaulted many years previously in the street by a Gentile who had thrown his fur hat into the mud. 'And what did you do?' asked Sigmund. 'I went into the roadway and picked up my cap,' answered his father (Freud, 1900a, p. 197). In this family story, Freud comes across suspension of reaction, protection from emotions, the transcribing of the trauma into a memory, and its narrative re-evocation in the context of the father–son relationship—a constellation of events that contains the science and the method of psychoanalysis.

Freud's father is not embarrassed by the humiliation he has undergone, as would have been the case in an aristocratic society and in a type of morality based on honour. He takes it for granted that it is impossible to resolve the conflict socially, since there is no mediation. Jacob Freud refers to times that were worse than his son's, times when Jews were denied citizenship and, consequently, legal protection and political representation.

The impossibility of expressing and generalizing conflict politically produces hypertrophy of the imagination, a constant transfer of the external to the internal, and the stupefaction of defence mechanisms, which alter the scene of events.

Freud writes in the 'Postscript to *An Autobiographical Study*' (1935a),

> I perceived even more clearly that the events of human history, the interactions between human nature, cultural development, and the precipitates of primarial experiences (the most prominent example of which is religion) are no more than a reflection of the dynamic conflicts between the ego, the id and the Superego, which psychoanalysis studies in the individual—are the very same processes repeated upon a wider stage. [p. 72]

Such a declaration, coming from a period at the end of Freud's working life, is a product of psychoanalysis itself. It would not be possible without the acknowledgement of the inner landscape, which was the result of thirty years of psychoanalytic therapy.

In this sense, there is justification for Lacan's paradoxical statement that the unconscious does not exist outside psychoanalysis, because it is an effect of its reasoning, a meaning induced by its signifier. 'The unconscious before Freud is *not* purely and simply'. Initially psychoanalytic science was identified with the self-representation of a minority, with its specific 'discontents in civilization', but it progressively widened its horizons of reference, both because other people identified with it and because it changed its referent. Early on in his research, in 1905, Freud had analysed in *Jokes and their Relation to the Unconscious* (1905c) the ways in which language deals with socially impracticable forces. The material was drawn from daily life in Jewish society and expressed the intertwining of social relations. The main characters are the *Schnorrer*, or poor man trying to scrounge a living, and the opposite figure of the millionaire, the marriage broker, the authoritarian father, the scheming mother, and the marriageable daughter. Through the game of double meanings (the puns of the *Witz*), Freud reconstructed the tensions and mediations of a social world. In the laughter, the irony, and the caricature it is possible to see the workings of compromises that allow people to render explicit—on the social scene—otherwise unrepresentable erotic and aggressive impulses. The calculations of social conventions become transformed into calculations of psychological conventions.

The mental apparatus takes on the onus of the conflict, processes it, and returns it to the world of interpersonal relations divested of its destructive properties. But for this to be possible there has to be a closely knit language community, a homogeneous socio-cultural context, and a shared intellectual style.

The understanding of a witticism (which always involves enjoyment of it) requires an identity of psychological structure between speaker and listener, a common heritage of experience, a form of pre-comprehension of the linguistic event, a shared feeling, and a unified traditional outlook.

In the witticism are produced metaphors that organize the meaning in such a way as to evoke unexpected referents, recognized as such, however, because they belong to the same world of symbols and the same outlook of expectation. The international success of Woody Allen—his comedy, which takes place totally within the realm of Jewish tradition—proves how the historical experience of the assimilated Jews is now universally shared, extended to western culture. The vision of the great Jewish mother obscuring the sky in the film 'New York Stories' illustrates the sharing of a particular cultural experience better than any reasoned argument.

However, assimilation does not prevent Jews from continuing to feel different, although this difference is becoming less and less explicit, almost impalpable. 'Who is Jewish?' Freud himself, who questioned himself all his life about his being Jewish, goes back—as we know, from when he was speaking to the members of the B'nai B'rith Association—to 'obscure emotional forces'. Yet the whole of the third essay in *Moses and Monotheism* (1939a [1937–39]) demonstrates that western civilization has assimilated Jewishness in the sense that it has identified with its requirements and introjected its deep structures—so much so that paradoxically the Jews seem to have been left behind by their history and are extraneous, through fixation, to the evolution of their own culture. By refusing to recognize themselves to be—like all men—murderers of God, they might be said to have missed out on the admission of guilt and the working-out of mourning. What Christians accuse them of, according to Freud, might be synthesized thus: 'They will not accept it as true that they murdered God, whereas we admit it and have been cleansed of that guilt', with the comment, 'It is easy therefore to see how much truth lies behind this reproach' (1939a [1937–39], p. 133).

Out of the opposition between Judaism and Christianity, Freud intended to extract that fragment of truth which stays intact in any form of delirium. And religions are, according to him, delirious constructs of humanity, which, in the form of denial or acknowledgement, go back to a fundamental event: the original murder. While the Jews, in denying this act, are offering themselves as scapegoats (since the lack of elaboration transforms them into a symptom of repression), psychoanalysis has elaborated a myth that allows the gap to be filled in, and the missing agnation and elaboration to be made up for. The world may be divided about the killing of Jesus, but as regards the killing of the chief of the horde in *Totem and Taboo* (1912–13), there are no possible defections. It fixes a valid origin *'erga omnes'*, because it precedes history, at the beginning of man's humanization, when differences of language or faith had not yet intervened.

Freud was so keen on eliminating the cultural reasons singling out Jews as victims that he even denied the genealogy of Moses and made him of Egyptian origin. He feared, and not without reason, that the specificness of history might be transformed into the inevitability of destiny.

The replacing of an origin myth giving rise to a people's peculiarity by an origin myth giving rise to the universality of the human race is made possible by the theoretical foundation itself of psychoanalysis. By making the prohibition of incest the keystone of the unconscious and of civilization, Freud opened up psychology to universality. In anthropology and metapsychology, psychoanalysis is presented as knowledge of human beings about human beings, legitimizing itself as the science of the individual and collective unconscious. In *Moses and Monotheism* (Freud, 1939a [1937-39]), we can see the attempt to supersede the relativeness of history by the introduction of elements of continuity, segments of repetition, and factors of permanence, presented by individual and institutional delirium as truths.

In ideological forms, Freud saw the distorted expression of truth that is more a logical necessity than a factual one.

He investigated, in the complex web of religion, a structure of possible events that can be understood, like the thoughts of dreams, only in its derivatives. To my mind, this going back to something else, to an atemporal dimension of events, is the apex of Freud's most tormented and unresolved work.

In this undertaking of the later stages of his life, we are aware of a moral and political urgency that cannot be immediately translated into conventional essay-writing.

All his reflections on Jewishness show traces of tension between the limits imposed by the present and the speculation solicited by the timelessness of the unconscious. In this sense, the myth of *Totem and Taboo* (1912-13) is only a hypothesis drawn up in a vacuum. But it does show that it is possible to rewrite history, to start again by voicing the truth and so render superfluous all the distortions of delirium and the 're-presentifications' of suppression. When Freud concluded *Moses*, it was the summer of 1938. The fascist racial laws were about to come out. The sinister shadow of Nazism was spreading over Europe, superimposing on the 'inner stage' a scene of destruction and death, which would make many feel 'like a Jew'.

This was the beginning of an emotional and cultural convergence of intellectuals and Jews, which would progressively lead to identification of one with the other and all too often, especially among psychoanalysts, identification on aesthetic principles. This convergence would be confirmed by the interest and consensus forming around Jewish culture.

Historically, Jewishness has been considered, he observes, as the emblem of a minority, in comparison with the universalistic vocation of Christianity and Islam. Now that the West has abandoned the claim 'to be the world' and is progressively considering itself to be only a part of it, it is finding new reasons for consonance in Jewish culture. The end of colonialism, the ceasing of evangelization, and the fall in the birth-rate have brought our civilization to the position of 'elite minority' that has distinguished Jewishness for centuries.

The loss of a global outlook is felt particularly by humanistically trained intellectuals, excluded from the centres of power and the distribution of wealth and forced to fall into line with the requirements of the industry of culture. Their fringe position in society is congruously represented by a form of thinking—like that of the Jews—that has derived new figures of universality from the very position of being only a part of it. In this sense the spread of psychoanalysis world-wide, and its very success, are in danger of bringing about a loss of identity. In the face of this, as if in a defensive move, the inner scene that is the chief object of analytical investigation tends to become self-referential and so interrupts Freud's close comparison with history and with human institutions. But the safeguarding of the specific nature of a form of knowledge lies not so much in orthodoxy as in the maintaining of a historical perspective. Bringing up the doubts and questions again about 'Psychoanalysis and Judaism' allows us to reconnect Freud's legacy to the hypotheses concerning its formation and the productiveness of its limits. Acknowledging the fruitfulness of psychoanalysis as something rooted in a decentralized minority culture increases its power to criticize and emancipate and causes it to make a critical evaluation of its own institutionalization, which is inevitable in any case. Allowing a cultural experience and a historical tradition to interact enables us to make up *culturally* for a *historically* imposed fringe position, for a 'non-belongingness' decreed in the name of genetics but interpreted in terms of criticism and a refusal of what exists. From this point of view, the Jew becomes a figure of ethics, a collector of tension, and an interpreter of unease—a bridge between the past of *arche* and the future of *telos*.

CHAPTER FIVE

Humour as a Jewish vocation and the work of Woody Allen

Cesare Musatti

Jewish witticisms, wrote Freud (1905c), 'know their real faults as well as the connection between them and their good qualities and the share which the subject has in the person found fault with creates the subjective determinant (usually so hard to arrive at) of the joke-work' (pp. 111–112). Here lies the difference between the witticism and the nasty joke. In Jewish humour the tension between the two registers—antisemitic accusation and Jewish self-defence—is enormous, to the extent that very little is needed to distort the meaning. But on a second reading, an analysis of the message reveals something more, aimed at the very basis of the accusation. And so the same joke, when told by non-Jews in a non-Jewish context, can have quite the opposite effect. The person who split his sides laughing at a joke told by

---

Musatti's contribution first appeared in 1982, in a collection of psychoanalytic essays subdivided into five sections, of which the third is entirely devoted to Judaism: *Mia sorella gemella la psicoanalisi*, pp. 128–139 (Rome: Editori Riuniti, 1982).

friends at their home the day before might easily feel uncomfortable at hearing the same joke elsewhere—in a cabaret, for example—and perceive the old, undying aggression towards the Jews in the audience's laughter.

Nor is this a mere reflection of the traditional, more than justified, Jewish hypersensitivity. The delicate nature of the witticism requires all the necessary elements to be present in order for its meanings to be fully conveyed. First of all it needs its own special audience, who know it is 'one of us' who is telling the joke, in a *'heimlich'* [familiar] context. Otherwise the joke, especially if it is one of the nastier kind, is liable to have its meaning distorted. Freud himself (Jones, 1953–57, Vol. 1), who was something of an expert on Jewish humour, once, in his old age, believed a sick joke against the Jews to be true. It concerned the Jews in Berlin under Hitler, who organized a demonstration with placards, saying, 'Throw us out'. On this occasion Freud vented all his grief and resentment against what he most condemned in German Jews, who were 'more German than the Germans'.

Many scholars have studied Jewish humour, starting from Freud (1905c, 1927d) who thought that humour was particularly relevant to understanding the Jewish cultural ethos. After Freud, every psychoanalyst, in his clinical practice or cultural reflection, has felt the need to confront himself with the problem of the meaning that should be conferred on humouristic communication in its multiple aspects. These are metapsychological aspects of defence from archaic anxieties, which would otherwise be unbearable, and aspects of the attempts that have been made to integrate and elaborate them (Reik 1929, 1954, 1962; Sacerdoti, 1988a; Meghnagi, 1989a, 1991).

Humourism presents a number of analogies with creative processes of literary and artistic genre.

In his re-evocation of the period when he was working during the 1930s on the preparation of the *Trattato di psicoanalisi* (Musatti, 1957), right in the middle of the antisemitic campaign, the pioneer of Italian psychoanalysis had occasion to remember the difficulty he found in looking for an analogous product in other cultures and the decision not to give any demonstrative example in the chapter on the *Witz*. Musatti distinguishes three types of Jewish humour: (1) the original humour of the ghettos and the Jewish forced residence areas; (2) that of the period of emancipation, of which Chaplin's cinema was to be the most representative (although Chaplin was not Jewish himself, all his themes are Jewish and were related to Jews); and (3) the cinema of Woody Allen, expressing a condition of confidence that is new and hitherto unknown to Judaism in the western world. The triumph of Woody Allen's films is evidence of the fact that Jewish historical experience has everything in common with his characters and situations.

Musatti's argument acquires greater relevance if one takes into account that in the early days of American cinema a Jewish director (this happened to William Wyler) was dissuaded from using in a film with a Jewish theme an actor who was too openly Jewish, such as Paul Munni. In America in the 1930s a Jew playing the part of a Jew could seem to be going just too far, and in a film in 1937 on the life of Zola, the reasons behind Dreyfus' persecution remained mysterious and unspecified. America had to wait until the end of the 1940s for the first two films openly denouncing antisemitism: 'Crossfire' and 'Gentlemen's Agreement'. Only from the 1960s onwards did American cinema put forward a new, proud, open image.

[ED.]

In the course of his working life, Freud dealt specifically with humour on two occasions: first, in 1905, in the book on the Witz (1905c) and twenty years later in the paper to the Innsbruck International Congress in 1927, entitled 'Humour' (1927d). Especially in the earlier work, which concerns not only humour, but also comedy and wit, Freud refers continually to story-telling, and hence to verbal expressions.

Cinematography was then in its early stages, and, apart from the so-called comics, all relying exclusively on movement, humorous situations could only be the object of the spoken or written word.

In the *Witz* (1905c), Freud took all his examples from Jewish stories, and almost always from the Jewish society of central and eastern Europe—Ashkenazim, we might say. Often the expressions themselves are in Yiddish, or translated from Yiddish. The *Witz* sold few copies, and Freud himself did not like it much, perhaps because it is too shamelessly Jewish and Freud was concerned that his brainchild, psychoanalysis, should appear as something purely scientific and not dependent on positions of partiality.

The book, as the title tells us, deals above all with the witticism. The scientific interest motivating Freud was not obviously literary, but regarded the psychic dynamisms that are set off: in other words, what happens inside ourselves when we either deliberately fabricate or, better, spontaneously produce a witticism, and also when we hear it from other people and enjoy it as well as laugh at it.

Freud was induced to relate the question of the witty joke to comedy in general, and also to humour. He even attempted a certain distinction, of a rather academic and abstract nature, between what is witty, what is comic, and what is humorous. He could not, however, avoid admitting that there are mixtures of two or three types and that sometimes the three situations, having as their effect the raising of a laugh (but perhaps a laugh that has very different shades of meaning), end up by interfering with each other.

Nevertheless, a certain differentiation can be made. As Freud writes, comedy is that which provokes a more elementary, cruder reaction and does not therefore require any refinement of thinking in the listener to provoke an impulse to laugh; whereas wit implies in the listener, and in the author himself, more complex processes and a similar identity of psychological structure between the two. Humour, on the other hand, reaches the highest point of dignity: it creates between the humorist and anyone who identifies with him an extraordinary understanding and unitedness.

A typical form of humour is, therefore, found in Jewish stories. And Freud, as we have already said, is careful to point out with some insistence that these are generally considered to be jokes that Jews themselves have made up, not those jokes told about them by Gentiles: the latter are mostly only concerned with emphasizing that which in the eyes of non-Jews is seen to be comic in Jewish habits and customs and may express the aggression that always develops towards those who are felt to be different from the majority community.

So Freud is particularly interested in the wit expressed by Jews towards themselves, or those who are considered to belong to the same group. This type of wit can be even more aggressive—subtly aggressive—than the crude stories coined by non-Jews, because ultimately only Jews know themselves thoroughly, know all the hidden corners of their personalities, including those that prudence, or sense of shame, and above all the eternal fear of antisemitism, would advise them not to wave about in front of strangers.

Freud considers that the Jewish stories, built up by the Galician and Polish Jews of his times, are particularly revealing of the special group characteristics that attract aggressive criticism from outsiders; and that they are the expression of the harsh, poverty-stricken life of Jews who depended on alms (extorted on the pretext of religious laws) from the few rich Jews (the so-called barons), which developed the art of scrounging—*schnorren*. Such stories would then constitute the essence and the origin of Jewish self-directed aggressive wit.

Even when their material conditions improved and Jews left their original, traditional state, this inner tendency to self-criticism could be said to remain. Self-critical wit can be identified with humour. Humour would result when the author, in rising above his poverty, weakness, and even cowardliness or cunning, himself makes his unhappy condition the object of laughter.

But why publicize one's negative qualities? Why expose oneself negatively in this way to strangers, making them laugh and becoming a humorous character? This is the secret of humour.

By ironically exposing his blemishes, weaknesses, and defects, the humorist stands to gain more than he loses in other people's consideration. 'And you, little man, who laugh at me and make fun of me, did you think you could discover all these things I suffer from? Don't you know I have always been aware of my burden of woes, complications, and anxieties?' So he succeeds in attracting a feeling of likeableness, sometimes of sympathy, but also admiration, so converting other people's aggression into solidarity. This is the tragic and dramatic aspect of real Jewish humour. Hence Freud talks about greatness of spirit, something of an elevated and ennobling nature in humorous behaviour.

As for the receiver of the humorous message, Freud describes thus the psychological process by which an intimate, specific pleasure is generated: he who is prepared to develop sympathy, or any other affection, even of a negative nature, for the character represented, or who represents himself, becomes suddenly aware that this affection is superfluous, because the character reveals himself to be superior to his misfortune and defects and is ultimately triumphant in a way. This 'sparing of affection' is one of the most frequent sources of humorous pleasure, according to Freud.

In his second essay of 1927, specifically devoted to humour, Freud eventually talks of humour as a 'triumph of narcissism' (1927d, p. 162) in the individual, an elevation of the persona. In fact, he adopts the new terminology introduced in his latest writings and states that the superego emphasizes itself at the expense of the ego. In the same way as when one falls in love and the ego empties itself of all its charge of libido, which is concentrated on the beloved, in the situation of humour the superego becomes inflated at the expense of the ego: this creates a situation that is connected with paranoia—delusions of grandeur. In this second, late essay, Freud, although without contradicting his previous statements, refrains from relating humour to Jewish thinking, as he had done in 1905. Nevertheless, I think he still had in mind and was always very aware of that vein of humour that is characteristic of Jewish society.

On the subject of Jewish humour—as well as the relationship with the social conditions of poor Jews, who were despised and persecuted, which is what Freud was thinking of in 1905 when he referred to the Central European Jews (especially those of his childhood and his family, who had originally come from Galicia and later emigrated to the Sudeten)—I believe another factor should be borne in mind.

Jews make jokes about themselves, in front of non-Jews: here there may certainly be, as Freud says, an attempt to convert their condition of supposed inferiority in strangers' minds to one of superiority, which is reached by elevating themselves and demonstrating that they are aware of, and in a certain sense able to dominate, their specific traits. But the Jews make jokes about themselves also, and especially among themselves, in situations where this need for redemption and the overturning of values should not be particularly necessary. Hence one is led to think that there must be some masochistic, self-attacking tendency, which is still the occasion for setting off a conversion of the minority condition into a feeling of superiority, but which derives from a genuine pleasure in describing these weaknesses of one's condition.

There are some who resolutely deny this masochistic component in Jewish humour—as, for example, Schlesinger, in an article written in 1979. However, it is difficult to understand how Jews would find pleasure so often in humour they themselves are the butt of, if this masochistic enjoyment were not present.

We have probably all known older relatives or friends of relatives whose principal occupation when the working day was over was to tell funny stories about the Jews: some of these were invented, others were drawn from real-life occurrences. But there are limits, and strong objections among Jews themselves, to this type of masochistic humour, which can revive the fear of antisemitism that has always remained an Achilles' heel for many Jews. So many are heard to exclaim: 'Stop it! That's enough! You have nothing else to talk about apart from Jews! We are no different from anyone else. We are just providing meat for antisemitism by talking like this!'

The question of Jewish humour—both of literary and, more recently, of cinematographic origin—is certainly, however, of great interest. At the same time, it is difficult to analyse, since it requires specific knowledge of Jewish society, which can be held only by those who become specialists in the subject; also, humour and jokes have the habit of losing their flavour when they are subjected to minute analysis. This destroys the element of 'surprise and terseness' that is essential to the dynamism at the root of humour. It is like a joke that is repeated or badly told and so becomes boring.

Bearing this in mind, as well as the fact that to draw valid conclusions it would be necessary to examine thoroughly a large quantity of literary and cinematographic material, which is unfortunately not available to me, I think that (starting off from Freud's comments on the subject which we have already mentioned) some observations about Jewish humour can be made.

One ought to begin, in my opinion, with a chronological distinction. There is classic Jewish humour, born in the ghettos, or at any rate in Central- and Eastern-European communities: the *Stätchen*, where life evolved in conditions of varying degrees of segregation. In this particular society—where the *Schnorrer*, the marriage-brokers [*Schadchen*], the *Hacham*, the rabbis gifted with prophetic qualities, all thrived among small trades-people living on their wits—Freud's observations on humour as an antidote to degradation and poverty are particularly valid. Emblematic of this type of bitter, tragic humour of oriental Jews, bereft of country and of hope, is the *Witz* (taken from Saint-Exupéry, but obviously dating back to the nineteenth century), which has formed the title for Claudio Magris's (1967) book about Joseph Roth: one Jew tells another he is about to set off for a far-off unknown country. The other says: 'You're going all the way there? How far away you'll be!' And the former replies: 'Far away from where?' This is a type of humour that is only verbal, much used in fiction, but rather difficult to use in theatre or cinema, owing to the lack of counterparts, or interlocutors.

We have to wait until the generation of Jews emigrating to the West produces a humorous character: the Jew living in an environment where the majority are Gentiles.

One condition of the transformation is that the Jews no longer live confined in a completely closed community, but have contacts with the rest of the world. Then the Jew becomes a lonely individual, one who is able, in conditions of misfortune, poverty, and privation, to use his personal character traits on the one hand and his ability to get through these difficult situations on the other, and so convert—by means of the comic devices he uses at his own expense—his misfortune into a state of being able to dominate the situation.

This is Chaplin's humour: the little man in his state of loneliness. In his films Chaplin (apart from 'The Dictator', where he himself is the Jew) never meets another Jew. Here the setting in which he is forced to operate, while he remains alone, has to be represented and acted out. Chaplin's humour, for example, cannot be *told as a joke; it must be seen* in his position against the world, to which he remains, in a certain way, a stranger. It is as if he were always trying to enter it, but without success. And since his films are silent, his humour is all a matter of gesture and uses the same technique, one might say, as the joke, which suddenly raises the protagonist from his state of apparent need for pity to a position of winner's superiority.

The transition of the cinema from silent to talking modified the situation a great deal. This can be seen even in Chaplin, whose greatest successes belong to the former period.

The talking film, by introducing dialogue (but also monologue), brings us nearer to classic Jewish humour and the *Witz*.

But the characters have also changed. They belong, so to speak, to the third generation: they are no longer the Jews of the ghettos or the Polish or Ukrainian *Stätchen*, nor even those who emigrated to the West or to that great and terrible country, the United States of America, where they found themselves alone in a totally strange environment. They are, instead, those of the following generation, who are genuine Americans even if still Jewish, and who are completely assimilated, like Woody Allen: a New Yorker living among other people, apparently quite amalgamated in the melting-pot of races, nations, and religions that is New York—only apparently amalgamated, however, since you only need to scratch a little to find his origins under the surface; and, in the case of Woody Allen, these origins are in no way concealed.

In one of this many-sided person's books (he is a writer, cinema script-writer, director, musician, and great actor) there is a whole chapter of Chassidic Jewish stories, which are certainly derived from a persistent family tradition or from a Chassidic spirit that is easily accessible because of shared ideas and thinking, apart from any differences of present-day living conditions. The variety of Allen's activities is also connected with this fundamentally unique hereditary outlook on life.

The truth is that he always represents the same character, for whom, in spite of the self-assurance and coolness deriving from his being part of this ruthlessly realistic environment, things don't always turn out well. And things go in such a way as to create the condition for humour—that is, there are weaknesses, defeats, failures, which the victim uses to redeem himself by revealing himself to others, yet showing himself to be superior to his misfortunes.

It can certainly be said that within any work of art there is something of the autobiographical, but in a work of art dominated by a humorous approach the autobiographical becomes obvious, since humour can only be created by using oneself.

The impression Woody Allen gives is always of really telling the story of his life. In 'Manhattan', for example, we see the complications arising from modern ways of understanding sexual and family relationships, so that we have a mixture of traditional relationships in the case of the son (when Allen goes and collects him, he plays ball with him and stops in front of the toy shop), the ambiguous relationship with his former wife, who has left him for a lesbian and who slanders him, and towards whom he has an ambivalent attitude of loving anger but also of a certain respect, the relationship with his friend's girlfriend, which turns out to be quite insubstantial, and the relationship with the girl who is in love but is just too young.

Yes, they are all true—or potentially true—stories, where it is always Woody Allen who is the victim of the situations he bravely tries to tackle, but which don't work out. But they don't work out only up to a certain point; he always manages to pull through in the end, even when it was he who got himself into the mess and risks making a fool of himself or appearing incapable.

Often the reference to classic Jewish humour in Allen's films becomes explicit, as in 'Take the Money and Run', when he goes mad and thinks he has become an oriental rabbi and behaves as such.

Not only does Woody Allen do nothing to hide his Jewishness, but he often puts it on show, as when in 'Manhattan' he talks about his father being forced, owing to Allen's financial difficulties, to content himself with a seat farther away from the Lord in the Synagogue, or refers to his mother as if she were a Zionist castrator.

Allusions such as these may make people laugh in Italy if they are acquainted with Jewish society, or they may escape the vast majority of the audience. But in the United States, where there persists a certain segregationism, if not outright antisemitism, these Jewish allusions of Allen's could be considered almost provocative. This shows how his humour is so self-confident that it can even attract feelings that risk turning hostile, with the confidence of someone who always remains the winner in the situation.

Even in his lighter films, Allen comes up again with racism, and also with psychoanalysis—of the kind that Freud called 'interminable analyses'.

Jewishness and psychoanalysis are undoubtedly connected, not only because of the nature of the founder of psychoanalysis, but because many psychoanalysts are themselves Jews or have Jewish connections. Thus Jewish humour can be related to the critical humour of which psychoanalysis is frequently the butt.

Technically speaking, there would certainly be much to say about Allen's neurosis and a psychoanalytical examination of it. He himself frequently repeats that psychoanalysis has not been very successful for him. But it has largely been substituted by his artistic activity, which has allowed him to let off steam about and resolve his negative transference towards the analyst, and to sublimate the elements of the neurosis in the creation of fantasy and humour.

In 'Annie Hall', Woody Allen says he has been going to his analyst for years for treatment of his neurosis and then exclaims: 'I'll keep on going for another year, and then I'll go to Lourdes.' So, in a single phrase, we have a humorous involvement of: the author, who personally reveals his neurosis; psychoanalysis, as a form of treatment that does not lead to a cure; and Lourdes, in which Allen shows he has just as little faith as in psychoanalysis and in himself.

PART FOUR

'MOSES AND MONOTHEISM'

CHAPTER SIX

The logic of Freudian research

Jorge Canestri

The author, who has been working for some years on the concept of 'figuration', proposes in this chapter to shed light on an essential aspect of Freud's epistemology—that of its being closely linked with inner experience. Canestri's paper discusses Freud's method of investigation and the significance to be attributed from this point of view to the presence of themes and reflections about Judaism in Freud's writing.

'Freud's writings', writes Canestri, 'have the merit of corresponding, usually, to the patients' own words. They preserve, to a great extent in some cases, substantial evidence of the processes giving rise to these accounts. They function as constructs that repeat [*Wiederholt*], in their "becoming", the motivational processes that oriented the author, the repressions and the returning of repressed object that conceded to hypothesis, and sometimes to myth and fiction, the place due to the supposed truth of what had been repressed, so following the rigid logic of deforming tendencies [*enstellenden Tendenzen*] that are constantly at work.' In this sense, the presence of Jewish fantasies in Freud's writings, like some of his rash investigations in other areas of the subject, may be re-interpreted, apart from the results obtained in the specific field being dealt with, as 'figurations' and 'exemplifying constructs' of a logic of research founded on the hybridization of scientific elaboration and literary elaboration, of speculative inclinations and merciless factual criticism, of reasoning and imagination, scientific reason and scientific imagination, the logic of discovery and the logic of justification: a synthesis that could be given the name, as the author concludes, of Lakatos's term, 'heuristics'.

[ED.]

The reference, suggested by the title, to the classic, although much-discussed, work of Karl Popper (1934) is certainly intentional. Well known is the distinction that the author borrows from Reichenbach (1935) between the 'logic of discovery' and the 'logic of justification': 'If we make a distinction, as Reichenbach does, between a "procedure for finding" and a "procedure for justifying" [a hypothesis] then we have to say it is not possible to reconstruct the former rationally.' This impossibility of inserting the 'procedure of finding' into the logical analysis of scientific knowledge is theorized by Popper as 'the elimination of psychologism' from the context of epistemology, since, although it can be admitted that the conception of a theory 'may be of great interest from the point of view of empirical psychology', 'it is my opinion . . . that there is no . . . logical method for obtaining new ideas, nor any logical reconstruction of this process (Reichenbach, 1935, Part 1, Chapter 1, Point 2: 'Elimination of Psychologism').

More than 40 years later, Imre Lakatos, although acting within the enlarged framework of the falsifying Popperian conception, was to contest the division made by the great master. In analysing the logic of mathematical discovery, Lakatos (1976) reveals a certain short-sightedness in Popper's approach. Lakatos says that when Popper (in 1934, in fact) divided the aspects of discovery into psychological and logical aspects, in such a way as not to leave any room at all for heuristics as an independent field of enquiry, he obviously did not notice then that his 'logic of discovery' was more than a mere *strictly* logical reconstruction of scientific progress. But Popper, who laid the foundations of this (fallible) logic of discovery, did not deal with the meta-question of what the nature of his enquiry was and did not notice that this is neither psychology nor logic, but an independent discipline, the logic of discovery, heuristics.

Lakatos's recognition of the existence of 'an intrinsic unit of logic of discovery and logic of justification' is, in the words of G. Giorello, 'an attempt to understand *those problems, those procedures by trial and error, those tactics and strategies of research* that make scientific practice as fascinating an activity as any creative activity (1976, italics added).

One must not, however, be misled into thinking that this means going back to psychological facts, to the pure invention of hypothesis, to the Kantian *'quid facti?'*, and to psychologism, all repudiated by Popper. Psychological facts could be analysed and interpreted according to the procedures of any form of psychology; theories could be considered along the lines of symptoms and become the object of psychoanalytical research; but all this, being pure psychology, would contribute nothing to the logic of research as conceived by Lakatos. Imagination, intuition, and invention can leave the domain of the indescribable if they are communicated, and nevertheless stay within the realm of the undecidable, no matter how the nature of scientific theories is conceived, which is the field of any epistemological current.

Lakatos's proposal states the need for the improvement of proof control procedures (logic of justification), which does not, however, exclude their being part of the same logic presiding over the discovery itself. This unity is given the name of heuristics, which has the task of comprehending the 'becoming' of science.

It is therefore in this perspective—which does not claim to say anything about the overall validity of any particular epistemology, but which acknowledges the preceding conception of Lakatos's to be substantially useful—that I propose to reflect briefly on the logic of Freudian research, to ponder the strategy that guided Freud throughout his life and work until his death.

For reasons of space a choice has to be made about which of the many elements characterizing this strategy should be given preference. Similarly, certain Freudian texts have been given preference over others (I attempted to consider other series of elements for analysis of the logic of Freudian research elsewhere—Canestri, 1985, 1986). As well as being famous for their literary quality, Freud's writings have the merit of corresponding, usually, to the patients' own words. They preserve, to a great extent in some cases, substantial evidence of the processes giving rise to these accounts. They function as constructs that repeat [*Wiederholt*], in their 'becoming', the motivational processes that oriented the author, the repressions and the returning of the repressed object that conceded to hypothesis, and sometimes to myth and fiction, the place due to the supposed truth of what had been repressed, so following the rigid logic of deforming tendencies [*entstellenden Tendenzen*] that are constantly at work.

One of these texts is probably *Moses and Monotheism* (1939a [1937–39]). This complex and contradictory work, untidy in form and in argument, whose historical bases are very shaky, reveals abundant evidence of all the pressing necessities that—it cannot be denied—compelled Freud to write it. We can therefore recognize the validity of the statement by Freud's biographer, Peter Gay (1988), when he says that to read it means participating in its construction.

One cannot help wondering why Freud, who was well aware of the shakiness and lack of balance of this work—so much so that he stated in the 'Prefatory Note II' (p. 299), written in London in 1938, that he was hesitant about his work because he felt it lacked that 'consciousness of unity and of belonging together which should exist between an author and his work'—was so determinedly keen on producing it and publishing it. And it must have been a case of real determination, bearing in mind the number of requests, and even threats, he received from all sources to discontinue his work and abandon his plans to publish it; moreover, he was struggling against the illness that was killing him, in a situation that was closing in on him, with Europe aflame with the spread of barbarity.

It is generally accepted that *Moses* is Freud's scientific response to the problem of antisemitism and racism, or, without implying any exclusion of the first hypothesis, that it is the result of an attempt to analyse the essence of Jewishness. With these and other hypotheses put forward in the now sizeable literature on the subject, I am essentially in agreement, and it is not my intention either to conjecture anything new or explore already existing conjectures. (Among the many valid essays devoted to the subject, I shall mention: Meghnagi, 1987a, Bakan, 1958, Robert, 1974, and Rubinstein, 1968.)

I should like, instead, to attempt to trace an outline of his research strategy, following the lead offered by some quotations of statements of Freud already familiar to scholars, and to produce a map, albeit incomplete, of the elements and forces in this strategy.

Taking a step back in time from the horror of Jewish persecution and the climate of impending war in 1938, we find ourselves in the midst of another horror, the First World War, which, as Freud foresaw, was merely the prologue to the next one. After a walk 'with a poet', he is inspired to make a brief, happy, and heartfelt observation. It is known to us by the title 'On Transience' (1916a), and it clarifies how war destroys not only the beauty of the world and its inhabitants, but also human pride in the progress of culture and civilization.

If we then return to 1938, we find Freud, who is about to go into exile in England, engaged in writing the first preface to the third part of *Moses*. There is no tenderness here, nor any mincing of words: 'We are living in a specially remarkable period. We find to our astonishment that progress has allied itself with barbarism' (1939a [1937–39], p. 54).

'The Progress of Intellectuality' [*'Der Fortschritt in der Geistigkeit'*] is the title of section C in the second part of the third essay in *Moses*, and the one that Freud entrusts to his daughter, Anna, so that it can be read at the International Psychoanalytical Conference in Paris on 1 August 1938.

This is a fundamental section of the essay, in which the author goes so far as to announce a *'new realm'*: the result of subordination of sensory perception to abstract ideas, which entails a renunciation of drive with 'all its necessary psychological consequences' (1939a [1937–39], p. 113). This process, which recognizes as an antecedent the development of language and the subsequent stimulus of intellectual activities, opens up to human beings 'the new reign of intellectuality in which ideas, memories and inferences became decisive in contrast to the lower psychical activity' (p. 113). If the reader remains in any doubt as to the importance of this detachment from 'matter' and 'materiality', this is soon eliminated by Freud with a specific reference to the 'material basis' of human existence. He says that even the act of turning to one's father and abandoning one's mother is a cultural progression, 'since maternity is proved by the evidence of the senses, while paternity is a hypothesis, based on an inference and a premise' (p. 114). It is therefore a case of the 'cogitative process' prevailing over that of sensory perception, which is implicit in the original term *'Geistigkeit'*, meaning also 'intellectuality'—hence the English translator's choice of 'intellectuality' rather than 'spirituality', with its religious connotations.

There is certainly no novelty in the hypothesis as a whole, which in fact will be very familiar to readers of Freud, who will no doubt remember the various stages of the course taken by Freud, starting with the *Project* and proceeding until the last of his works. He is faithful to the general analysis concluded in the complex summary written in 1911, 'Formulations on the Two Principles of Mental Functioning' (1911b). The essence of the argument is the necessary and desirable transition from the pleasure principle, a primary operating function of the psychical apparatus, to the principle of reality, since 'a system living according to the pleasure principle' must have organizations [*Einrichtungen*] 'that are merely the correlative [*Korrelat*] of repression' (1911b, p. 220, note 4). Thus the place of repression is taken by impartial judgement [*unparteiische Urteilsfällung*], which must decide whether a representation is true or false—that is, whether or not it agrees with reality [*'Realität'*— not the real external world, *'reale Aussenwelt'* or *'Wirklichkeit'*, since the decision is determined by the need to make a comparison with the mnesic traces of reality: *'Realität'*].

Outlined in this way, in what Freud called a justified fiction [*Fiktion*], and being unable to limit itself to satisfaction obtained through hallucination, the psychic apparatus has to turn to the workings of thought [*Denkarbeit*]. The thought processes [*Denkprozess*], originally mere representations [*blosse Vorstellen*], have the task of ensuring—in their increasing complexity and refinement and in the different figures they will be able to invent—that there are new plans and pathways, the only ones able to grant the subject a share of renewed pleasure. This is obtained through suitable modification of reality (Canestri, 1988).

This is the basis of Freud's hypothesis for explaining the progress of intellectuality: the privilege accorded to the function of thought processes guarantees, through renunciation [*Versagung*] of a momentary pleasure, the creation of new ways of ensuring a subsequent more certain one and creates the settings that characterize human culture, including art and science.

If this subject had previously been developed exhaustively, why did Freud return to it with renewed vigour and hand it over to his daughter as a sort of testament addressed to the psychoanalysts gathered for the Conference? What was there that was new in this work? There are certainly no new general ideas about religion. We know that Freud gave up the idea of writing a specific chapter on the theory of religion, although one may be misled by the many references to both the Jewish and the Christian religions. If they draw more analytic attention, it is essentially because they contribute evidence, among other things, of the progress of intellectuality which Freud was investigating.

The Mosaic religion, by forbidding representation, induces subordination of sensory perception to abstract ideas, determines an acknowledgement of spiritual powers with 'powerful effects', and gives rise to a form of ethics of high values. But through not confessing to the suppressed murder, this religion is reduced 'to some extent [to] a fossil' (Freud, 1939a [1937–39], p. 88) and draws the hate of other peoples onto those who practise it.

The Christian religion has confessed and is therefore one step ahead as concerns the return of the suppression, but it has also taken steps backwards. It is regressive, not strictly monotheistic, and preserves within itself magical and mystical elements that act as obstacles in the spiritual/intellectual development of mankind.

The analyses Freud has left to us are weak, and although they are suggestive and full of interesting ideas, they do not stand up to close historical examination and suffer from defects deriving from the rather doubtful validity of extending psychoanalysis freely to other areas. And yet, as has been said above, they are valuable in that they allow us to investigate this conception of Freud's in some depth and are the basis of his research strategy. In addition, as has been mentioned, we have an alliance between progress and barbarity. How was this possible? In this case, too, Freud tells us nothing new. The essential principle of a possible explanation, in terms of the psychic apparatus, had already been formulated and theorized with some clarity in *Group Psychology and the Analysis of the Ego* (1921c). This dealt with the corruption and degradation of the ego ideal—the opposite process to that of the progress of intellectuality; again, it is the latter that has become the centre of research. [This idea may be formulated in other ways that agree in essence with what is being expressed here, although they are slightly different. Compare the studies by D. Meghnagi, J. F. Winter, and P. Lacoue-Labarthe & J. L. Nancy, in Meghnagi, 1987a.]

But *Moses* is also, as I admitted earlier, a scientific work on the essence of Jewishness, on the 'mystery of the Jewish essence', on the mystery of the essence of the author of *Moses*, who was himself a Jew.

This essence, which is indissolubly linked to the most intimate identity of Freud himself (1941e [1926]), does not yield easily to analysis, and one may, to my mind, be allowed to doubt that his efforts produced results that are in any way conclusive. I do not, however, intend to examine them. I should like, instead, to consider the premises that provided the starting point for this quest for essence. These emerge quite clearly in some statements by Freud. In 1925 he wrote a letter to the Editor of the *Judäische Presszentrale, Zurich*, saying (Freud, 1925b):

> I can say that I stand as far apart from the Jewish religion as from all other religions: that is to say, they are of great significance to me as a subject of scientific interest, but I have no part in them emotionally. On the other hand I have

always had a strong feeling of solidarity with my fellow people.

The essence, then, does not depend on religion, which is in fact free from any emotional significance. This is not the case with the Jewish people, with whom there is a bond (in the psychoanalytic sense) that is impregnated with sentimental value. What starts off the need for a profound analysis, therefore, is the recognition of the existence of a component of the inner life—a component that in fact belongs to the very nucleus of the inner self and one that has not been sufficiently worked out.

In the 'Address to the Members of the *B'nai B'rith*', he again considered the question, which first and foremost related to himself, using similar words (Freud, 1941e [1926]):

> what bound me to Jewry was . . . neither faith or national pride. . . . But plenty of other things remained over to make the attraction of Jewry and Jews irresistible—many obscure emotional forces, which were the more powerful the less they could be expressed in words, as well as a clear consciousness of inner identity, the safe privacy of a common mental construction.

If compared to the preceding letter, the 'Address' adds a concept that is habitual to the author and to psychoanalysts: the relationship between the power of an emotional force and its expression in words. The resolution to go in search of this expression is implicit, and in his ability to recognize the powerful dark forces of emotion and to find a way of expressing them verbally with scientific dignity, we can identify one of the pivotal points of Freud's logic of research. This logic differs from the logic of enlightenment—which many have insisted is equivalent to Freudian logic—mainly in its starting point: reason is born in the unconscious.

When in 1930 Freud wrote the Preface to the Hebrew edition of *Totem and Taboo*, he formulated 'the question of his Jewish essence' in precisely the same terms as before. If someone were to ask him, he writes, what is there left that is Jewish, he would reply: 'A very great deal, and probably its very essence. He could not now express that essence in words; but some day, no doubt, it will become accessible to the scientific mind' (1934b [1930]).

On the basis of phrases such as this, Freud is commonly credited with great epistemological optimism. While not denying the effective existence of this (there are several indications of it in his works), I am inclined rather to see in statements such as these either strategic specifications for psychoanalytical research or the ethics that orientate this research. If one were to ascertain the existence of the ethics of research in psychoanalysis, the core problem would have to be identified with this tension that furthers, by scientific means, the recognition and ceaseless transformation of what is most secret in a subject.

And it is precisely the existence of an unceasing, restless process, explicitly desired by Freud, that allows the analysis of the essence of Jewishness to be thought out and eventually written in *Moses*, the last stage of Freud's self-analysis. The self-analysis that had begun with the acknowledgement of the Oedipus complex and had continued throughout the years and the vicissitudes of his life and his theories leads, finally, to the 'obscure emotional forces' that form the bases for the writing of *Moses*.

While the theoretical framework built up in the meantime enabled Freud to identify with the phrase written by Descartes to Mersenne, 'My method of analysis of the nature and properties of curves has gone beyond ordinary geometry, in the same way as Cicero's rhetoric goes beyond children's ABC', the final years of his life and the relentless uproar of madness spreading throughout the world counselled a return to delving into childhood babbling—because here something remained, an *'Ur-reste'*, on which depended essential forces to be analysed, forces that contributed to fostering the logic of research that had given meaning to his project, forces that had nourished his ethics, the ethics of psychoanalysis.

And he finds Moses the Egyptian, 'creator of the Jews', to all appearances the antithesis of Oedipus the Greek, to be merely an ersatz figure, or an alternative illustration of a fundamental constituent principle of the subject's nature, as he had represented him.

This is an exile, or rather an Exodus, with or without the capital E, meaning *ex-hodos*: a way out. Because Freud, a follower of Sophocles, makes Oedipus's blindness the condition for the opportunity of gaining knowledge, and exile the circumstance to which the 'return home' is subordinated. Or, alternatively, Freud, as a follower of Jewish history, makes the exiled person's fringe condition—his otherness, in comparison to ideological, national, and religious norms—a necessary quality for the progress of intellectuality, a quality that is doubly valuable in psychoanalysis if a position of participation during detachment has to be built up.

The exodus becomes, then, a point of contact for Greek, Jewish, and psychoanalytic interpretations of truth.

The annexing of Austria to Germany forced Freud into real physical exile. In London, where he was warmly received and treated as a welcome guest, and where he was free from Nazi oppression, he wrote a second preface to the third essay of *Moses*. Out of this I have extracted another idea to follow up, the last in this outline for a map of the symbolic driving forces defining the logic of Freudian research. He wrote: '. . . I am once more able to speak and write—I had almost said "and think"—*as I wish and as I must*' [*wie ich will oder muss*] (italics added). Peter Gay makes the acute observation that Freud may be a free man, 'but is not free to stop writing about Moses'. However, the remark need not be limited to *Moses*, putting it into the category of an isolated obsession and of a deviation from Freud's works in general.

Moses may be an 'invention', as Freud himself declared, but it is part of a large group to which scientific fantasies, theoretical fictions, conventions, scientific myths, and speculative inclinations also belong. The construction made evident in the preceding phrase applies to all of these.

What strikes one in Freud's second Preface is precisely the sense of constriction, of having to say or write, which is made even more vivid by the clashing contrast with his declaration of new-found freedom.

Evidence of the fact that this method of working, based on the need to give expression to what is pressing in one's mental experience, is a special, distinctive feature of Freud's 'procedure for finding' can be produced by turning our attention briefly to a letter Freud (1907–26) later wrote to Ferenczi about the 'Philogenetic Phantasy', which Freud had sent him. One section of the letter expresses the problem of a working method: *'Ich halte darauf, dass man Theorien nicht machen soll—sie müssen einem als ungebetene Gäste ins Haus fallen, während man mit Detailuntersuchungen beschäftig ist'* ['I am keen to point out that one should not make theories: they should turn up at one's home like unexpected guests, while one is busy with investigating particulars']. The sense of obligation [*müssen*], 'should happen', could be rendered by: they should impose themselves . . . like uninvited guests. In a way, therefore, that is analogous to the way in which fantasies impose themselves, in the psychoanalytic sense of the term.

That fantasies, and therefore also the theories that are unexpected guests of the mind, should also be controlled, is something Freud himself states explicitly in another letter to Ferenczi (Freud, 1907–26), describing the mechanism of scientific creativity as a 'succession of bold fantasy and merciless criticism exercised by reality'.

These are only some of the many indications provided by Freud for the building-up of a method of research hinging on the hybridization between scientific and literary elaboration, between speculative inclinations and merciless factual criticism, between reasoning and fantasy, between scientific reason and scientific fantasy (imagination)—in short, between the logic of discovery and logic of justification, which might be summed up in Lakatos's term 'heuristics'.

The logic of Freudian research is contrary, in many respects, to the division made by Popper and has much more in common with Lakatos's unitary proposal, since Freud explicitly admitted, and assumed as guiding principles, those fantasies that led him to the task of proving them (the *'müssen'* [obligation] mentioned above). He reveals the knots, the inner necessities, that guide him and suggest to him a certain strategy or route to take. He raises the 'obscure emotional forces' and desire to the position of material to be dealt with and dissected. But proving all this is, as has been said above, an obligation, another 'müssen', which is parallel and complementary to that which leads him to self-analysis. And in the field of providing proof, Freud behaves according to Lakatos's motto: 'improving proving', even when proving may not hit the mark, or may be wrong.

In *Moses* Freud offered us a final example of the significance of his enterprise—an enterprise and a battle brought to an end by his death more than fifty years ago.

PART SIX

APPLIED PSYCHOANALYTIC STUDIES

CHAPTER SEVEN

Psychoanalysis between assimilation and proselytism

Giorgio Sacerdoti

In the wake of studies by Rothman and Isenberg, this chapter distinguishes three ways of escaping from a condition of marginality. The first is the attempt to mix with the majority group and to deny one's specific existence. This, at the level of analysis in particular, is the attitude of those who tend to water down the most uncomfortable truths of psychoanalysis so as to make them more acceptable. The second tendency is to undermine from the inside the false certainties and prejudices of the dominant group—an attitude adopted by Freud at the scientific level against the prejudices and values of his time. The third operation is to transform the minority into the majority. In order to evaluate the degree of internal validity of each operation, the author proposes as a reference the proof of reality. Historically speaking, for example, any line of reasoning involving denial of its own Jewish identity had tragically led a section of contemporary Judaism, especially among the Jews of German culture, to a loss of contact with reality, both internal and external, and, in the most extreme case, to rejection and 'self-hatred' (the most tragic case being that of Otto Weininger). In the case of the culture of the Enlightenment, with its inability to accept real Jews, and not only the abstract picture of them, the situation led Jews towards a form of 'soft guilt-finding', as well as to incomprehension of the underlying mechanisms of the very logic of anti-Jewish feeling and of modern anti-semitism, with its strictly political character. Sacerdoti identifies the second attitude as being that of psychoanalysis. As a Jew, Freud always openly acknowledged his closeness to his people and sought to identify in Moses the cultural and psychological roots of the historical evolution that had led Jews to be what they were and to look for explanations for the unjust hostility towards them in the society of that time. Extending the subject to the discipline created by him, Freud never believed in the possibility of transforming psychoanalysis into a majority through an operation of proselytism. From this point of view, Sacerdoti ponders on the meaning of the spread of psychoanalysis during the past twenty years in Italy and in the West in general, and how much of this spread obeys the logic of projective assimilation, tending to empty Freud's work of its contents. The author also wonders to what extent a sort of more or less unconscious complacency of psychoanalysis itself, or of writers representing it, has contributed to a shift in direction of avoidance of marginality by adopting the first method.

[ED.]

After witnessing the requests for analyses for educational purposes with which training analysts have been bombarded for some years now, one cannot get away from one element in particular, which (leaving aside a whole series of others) is the object of our interest here: I refer to the fact, or impression, of finding oneself up against a sort of proselytism taking place between a certain proportion of these applicants and an image of psychoanalysis to which at least a certain proportion of analysts must in some way have contributed.

Since I propose to attempt to outline a definition of this phenomenon and its connections with assimilation, I must therefore briefly summarize what I tried to state in psychoanalytic terms in a previous study (Sacerdoti, 1987).

In psychoanalysis the word 'assimilation' is used fairly frequently, with regard both to the process of development and to the process of analysis. It seems, for various reasons, to cover different operations, which correspond more often than not to an unreal image of the assimilation process. If one refers to a physiological process, we have a model whereby parts of an object become similar to it: this model would correspond, in all but the place where this occurs, to 'projective identification', rather than to introjective identification or just plain identification. In psychoanalysis, on the other hand, when referring to assimilation, even when the digestive–metabolic model is emphasized, we talk about a process that refers not so much to the real physiological one as to a metaphorical one, such as is expressed in *'Man ist was man isst'* [we are what we eat]. Thus, according to Freud (1933a), the metamorphosis of the parental relationship into the superego is

> the so-called 'identification', that is to say, the assimilation [*Angleichung*] of an ego to an extraneous ego, in consequence of which the first ego behaves in certain aspects like the other, imitates it, and somehow absorbs it into itself. Not inopportunely, identification has been compared to the oral cannibalistic incorporation of an extraneous person. [p. 63]

Again in my previous study I noted that on the basis of clinical and anecdotal material, the watershed between the defensive and the evolutional character of 'projective assimilation' is marked by a test of reality. I also emphasized how the dynamics of assimilation can be better specified in their intrapsychical and interpersonal aspects and how one can avoid the risk of falling into error by using, instead of the noun ('assimilation'), the verb form ('assimilate'), which enables us to indicate through the form whether we have a transitive, prevalently active or passive operation, or a reflexive operation. By adding the adverb 'introjectively' or 'projectively', we can specify where the operation takes place and also, usually, its meaning: 'assimilating introjectively' means making oneself similar to another, and 'assimilating projectively' means making the other similar to oneself.

I should now like to digress briefly to gather together some of the characters of those involved in the dynamics of proselytism, and in particular the characters of the analysts; I shall take the liberty of doing so in the form of fiction. I shall imagine that we unexpectedly come across some psychoanalysts with a surprisingly similar position to that of certain psychiatrists who think it is possible to consider nothing but the unconscious. Working along the lines of a 'phylogenetic fantasy', one would wonder from whom such a species of analyst might be descended. From Freud? If so, they would then be neo-Freudians who are at the same time post- and pre-Freudians. We shall therefore call them, for the moment, 'post-pre-Freudians'. It is perhaps a case of a subspecies selected at a time when parthenogenesis was possible. Certainly they would require careful description. For the time being, let it suffice to say they have a certain preference for patients with sizeable 'psychotic' elements and pay particular attention to their mental attitude, in such a way as, among other things, to encourage perception, particularly of extra- or pre-verbal expressions. A description of their experiences by these analysts would give the impression that they were not only near the promised (or 'unknown') land, but that some of them had gone well over the boundaries—for example, certain limitations connected with the difference in sex between analysts and patients, which even Freud (1931b) humbly admitted were based on transference, on the subject of his knowledge of 'the dark continent'.

One wonders, as we bring this 'phylogenetic' tale to an end, whether these analysts—who are more realistic than the 'King' himself—might be connected with Freud/Hannibal (certainly not with Freud/Moses). In the above-mentioned selection there might have been more susceptibility as regards the possibility that psychoanalysis (which is already predisposed, so to speak) could be seen as 'projectively assimilable' by those who, animated by desires of omnipotence, actually project these desires onto the science that discovered the unconscious, by making this science at first an instrument (or at least a firm promise) for the recovery of the completeness that was lost at the time of primary separation (see also Chasseguet-Smirgel & Grünberger, 1979). Sooner or later, however, psychoanalysis itself will become a target for aggression associated with the other extreme—that of delusion. Or else . . . or else, if, among other things, desires of proselytism also come into play among analysts, it may happen that psychoanalysis, unlike what happened in the past, is reduced to impotence (and/or omnipotence) by means of that operation which, as already mentioned, I had attempted to indicate as being assimilated projectively. In this case psychoanalysis and certain psychoanalysts would become the object, rather than the subject, of proselytism—unless the 'projective assimilation', instead of taking the more numerous ways, which have in any case a defensive outcome from the inside point of view and an offensive outcome from the point of view of relationships, takes the way of an evolutional outcome, both at an intra-group and an inter-group level (by analogy with what may be deduced from clinical examples at an intra- and inter-individual level).

A curious thing I learned at the Egyptian Museum in Turin may perhaps re-introduce the concept and the games of assimilation in another way. A wealthy person of the Saitic period (600 B.C.) had had a sculpture made of himself in the act of holding a magic stele in front of him in order to make unification with the saviour god more tangible. Water was poured over the stele and the statue and so became impregnated with magic power before being administered to a sick person (compare baptism and God made Man, with the double transition from the word to the flesh [*Verbum Dei caro factum est*] and from the flesh to the name [*et Christus nomatum est*]). The reference is to the myths of a pricked or bitten deity, who is healed through the intervention of another god. The latter recites a magic charm, which has an immediate effect, and this formula could also heal the patient when repeated, the patient being assimilated [*sic!*] into the wounded deity. In other words, the god could—without any apparent need for a projective operation, which he could represent the basis for—be assimilated projectively into the patient simply because he was wounded. The other deity (which might represent the separated intact part of the divine figure) would then be introjectively assimilated—through the wounded figure or part that allows the assimilation (the greater the difference, the more likely are the rejection reactions).

Rothman and Isenberg (1974), in attributing to Freud the awareness of his fringe state of Jewishness, are perhaps suggesting that the new discipline of psychoanalysis, by establishing a universalistic psychology, was denying the reality of culture and cultural differences. According to these authors one of the first ways of escaping from a fringe state would be to assimilate oneself into the majority culture: something—we might say—half-way between being projectively assimilated and pure, 'spontaneous' assimilation in which appropriation, rather than the more frequent expropriation, is emphasized in the assimilating person (see, for example, Devoto & Oli, 1975). As a second way of escaping from a fringe state, the same authors propose attempting to undermine the dominating culture; a third way is to try and transform oneself and one's group into a majority. They recall that Freud sometimes considered religious conversion, but always rejected the idea; and that on the other hand he hesitated to adopt the Zionist ideology (which might correspond to the third way of escaping from a fringe state).

As regards the idea of the spread of psychoanalysis, I think it can be claimed that Freud was always fully conscious—apart from desiring it to be the case—that the movement would not be transformed into a majority through proselytism (for example, in psychology and in psychiatry) in any of the abovementioned ways, with the possible exception of the second (undermining the dominant culture), if one is to give any value to the joking phrase used by Freud on the occasion of his visit to America when he compared the advent of the culture of psychoanalysis to the introduction of the plague.

Freud also had broad but limited ideas on the subject of applied psychoanalysis (Sacerdoti, 1988b). And one might perhaps note that also in this field the mass of contributions has developed in inverse proportion to creativity.

It is perhaps not surprising that the mass of followers might become so (or develop) also in inverse proportion to the development of ideas. In this category might also be included certain approaches, such as Meltzer's (1986) extended metapsychology, for example, for which success in proselytism seems inevitable, at least in Italy: similarities with psychoanalysis would then be preserved by projectively assimilating psychoanalysis into such an 'extension'. This might be a topical matter of interest in reference to the theme of the next I.P.A. Congress, in the sense that common fundamentals in psychoanalysis imply that the territory is not unlimited.

CHAPTER EIGHT

Psychopathology of everyday antisemitism

Antonio Alberto Semi

> In his essay Semi deals with a particular aspect of anti-Jewish prejudice, the kind that is expressed in little gestures—gestures that are perhaps quite 'innocent' and abound in everyday life; not outright antisemitism, but the off-hand remarks and misunderstandings that may derive from the fact that a non-Jew bears an evocative surname; antisemitism as the expression of a desired inconfrontability between the two sexes, between different generations, and different cultures. Freud's theory that in antisemitism there lies an unresolved phantasm regarding origins, more specifically regarding the question of parricide, is examined and tested here in some clinical situations characterized by the emergence of the phantasm of Jewishness and anti-Jewishness in connection with unresolved Oedipus and pre-Oedipus problems, and by the attempt to avoid conflict by renouncing thought and the setting up of 'sado-masochistic' relationships.
>
> [ED.]

Reference to the famous passage from *The Interpretation of Dreams* (Freud, 1900a, p. 197), the one that is connected with Freud's identification with Hannibal and that marks one of the crucial points in Freud's self-analysis, is made here at the beginning of a brief discussion on everyday antisemitism in order to show how different the reading of this passage may be after Auschwitz. 'My father', said Freud, 'told me this story to prove how much much better things were now than they had been in his days'—is there not a double dose of irony nowadays in this passage?

Another reason for beginning with this historic reference, however, is that an important characteristic of everyday antisemitism consists precisely in its historical continuity, like a sort of little irritating symptom that is difficult to change—it could be compared to nail-biting, for example—which is a sign of something else that could explode into something much stronger at any given time.

My chapter is devoted to little episodes, even smaller than the one quoted, which only rarely involve immediate consequences—such as when, for instance, not many years ago in Venice it was discovered that the reason for the delay in approving a decision concerning a colleague lay in the hesitation on the part of an official in the Prefecture, who wanted to know whether the politicians who had made the decision were aware of the fact that the man in question was Jewish.

But let us return to the theme—a theme that might be said to be typically Italian. It is often argued that Italian antisemitism is not comparable to that of other countries. Often, in fact, such reasoning leads to the conclusion that after all, on a closer look, it is not really antisemitism at all and that the Italian people are so tolerant, mature, humane, good-natured, and so on that there have never been any particularly brutal manifestations of antisemitism, even when, so to speak, the right opportunity for such occasions presented itself—a country of saints, not to mention navigators and heroes. Personally, I consider Italian antisemitism to be somewhat superficial, although this is in no way an ennobling factor.

I ask you therefore to understand the expression 'everyday antisemitism' in the sense of 'antisemitism expressed through little gestures in everyday life'—that is, to understand this expression as a condensed way of emphasizing an analogy between the psychopathology of everyday life—whose revealing character has been taught to us by Freud (1901b)—and 'Italian-style' antisemitism, which is generally expressed through small things, fantasies, jokes, wilful ignorance, slips, little gestures of rudeness or of exaggerated politeness—in other words, phenomena that, when considered singly and in their own contexts, be it a conversation, a casual encounter, an introduction, a chat at the barber's, seem to have no value in themselves, so that it seems almost excessive or even suspicious to attach importance to them.

I shall return at the end to the apparent innocuousness of this type of antisemitism: let it suffice to say at the moment that as a result of the effects of fascism and its martial laws the tiny Italian Jewish community fell from 58,000 people registered in December 1938 to 26,000 in 1946, having lost about a quarter of its members in concentration camps and another third through forced emigration.

However, as regards everyday antisemitism, I feel I should first of all emphasize how the analogy suggested by the title implies a basic tenet of mine: that I believe it to be a valid argument to consider antisemitism in the light of psychopathology. This does not mean that there is any less responsibility on the part of the antisemites, but it does allow us to try to understand their attitude. And while we are on the subject of analogies, let me allude to a surprising analogy to be found among the studies and discussions on antisemitism as well as those on alcoholism.

When talking about alcoholics, psychiatrists frequently attach importance to the drinking habits of their patients: whether they drink wine or spirits, in what quantities and what sort of quality, at what rate, and so on. Alcoholics equally frequently put the blame for their having been brought to ruin on the wine itself. The conclusion is always the same: alcohol has to be eliminated in any case. The more informed psychiatrists and those psychoanalysts who have studied the problem have shown clearly that this talking about alcohol is a distraction, and the alcoholic does not become any the less an alcoholic merely by cutting out drink. But for us it is interesting to observe that, analogously, the literature on antisemitism is often devoted to the study of the characteristics of Judaism and that sometimes it in fact reaches the conclusion that, in order to solve the problem of antisemitism, all it needs is for Jews to be assimilated in one way or another.

This analogy lends itself to paradoxical conclusions: for example, although I don't know what Sartre's drinking habits were, his reasoning on the subject of antisemitism (1954), however noble in its intentions, would certainly induce one to think that he would have liked to eliminate alcohol, without being able to.

In accordance with the consequences of this analogy, I shall talk here about wine as little as possible, since it seems to me that the problem of antisemitism lies primarily in the antisemites. That these people exist and that there are many of them, I have been able to ascertain on some singular occasions: behind the writing of this chapter, besides the kind invitation on the part of the organizers of the seminar to which it was presented, there lies a series of misunderstandings, slips, false acknowledgements, dreams and associations of patients, which throughout my professional career have often amused me, sometimes worried me, but always interested me—little phenomena connected with my surname, which, because of its sound, leads people to link it with something Jewish (Semi: Semite, antisemitism, Semitic peoples, the Jews) and to suppose, accordingly, that I am Jewish myself.

This is no chance connection, if one thinks that only rarely have I happened to hear a link made with my surname and the field of botany, with which it would be equally easy to connect it in Italian: it could be one of the many Italian names of agricultural origin or symbology, a cognate of *semenza* [seed], *semenzato* [sown, disseminated], *arbore* [arbour], *rosai* [rose-tree], *della rovere* [oak-wood], and so on.

As a psychoanalyst, it is no great distress to me that this attributing of identity to me betrays a figment of illusion; after all, it is all part of my work. However, it is also part of my work to question myself about this series of incidents and their significance. And this is my theme: to see whether this lesser antisemitism—which is often latent and sometimes emerges to the serious embarrassment of those who discover it in themselves and who are not consciously antisemitic—has anything to tell us about antisemitism as we generally understand it, the egosyntonic version, and to expound some of the questions I have asked myself.

Before examining a couple of slightly more complicated cases—but which are also more useful in an attempt to put together an explanation of these phenomena—I could perhaps give some examples from everyday life, such as the very telling error made several times by some of the nursing staff at the psychiatric hospital where I worked: there was another psychiatrist with an obviously Jewish surname working in the same hospital, and I was often called by his name, and he by mine. This was a slip that was as curious as it was recurrent. As far as we could observe, this error cropped up whenever there was some reason for tension towards me or towards him.

Such examples may be common enough but are also relatively useless: more interesting are those that came up during analysis, because there it is possible, sooner or later, to try to understand the underlying causes.

So, in the course of my work, I once chanced to have a patient who had a tendency to incur debts and who was trying to tell me that he would not pay for his sessions with me. He said, referring to a tradesman from whom he had bought, but not paid for, some articles he did not need anyway, that this person was (his actual words) 'a really stingy character, a money-grabber, he's probably a Jew . . . oh, I beg your pardon!' I realized he was certain that I was one and was hoping I would be ashamed of this and would therefore show myself to be very generous by giving him the analysis for free.

Another patient, a woman, whom I shall discuss at greater length, began her analysis by lying on the couch and saying with a snort: 'I wonder what my father would have said, he who was so much of a fascist, if he had known I was going to spend his money lying on a Jew's couch.'

She is a woman of 40, educated, intelligent, and sensitive. She had asked for the analysis, with good reasons, after telephoning a centre for psychoanalysis, and had learned that statutory practice allowed only people under 40 to begin psychoanalytic training. Also, as far as I can ascertain, she asked for the analysis to be done by me—I am not a training analyst.

After a year of analysis, the patient, who sometimes alluded to a possible complicity with me, once began, during a session that later was seen to be important, to talk about a congress held by her political party, which she had attended; in so doing, she gradually wove a pattern under my very eyes—or rather, ears—with three continuously intertwining themes. One was concerned with herself, where the previous night she had been hungry and irritated and had drunk some wine so as to get to sleep. The second theme concerned important people—a politician, a hospital consultant, and a professor—all characterized by the fact that they let children suffer or cause them to suffer. A third theme developed from a singular chain of associations: there is a child who would like to sing but who is stopped by his parents from going to a music college; then a childhood memory of herself going to a music college to have lessons with a Jewish teacher, who told her to 'swell out her breast' (and the patient considers she does not have the large breast that prima donnas once had); then Primo Levi; and, finally, the works of Freud. From this chain of associations it can be understood how the patient fears—but is also resigned to the idea of—'singing', which in Italian also means 'telling tales'—telling tales, that is, to me, a Jew, even though she does not, and she even emphasizes this through the image of one of her heads of department, 'who always agrees with everything anyone says', thus indicating her desire to keep her distance from everyone.

During another session, a dream referring to a political demonstration held in two adjoining public squares by Israelis and Palestinians shows how this agreeing with everything anyone says (even when it is a case of events concerning objects 'in two different squares') represents the fulfilment of a desire to stay in a neutral position, even as regards her attitude to sex.

Her position during analysis is one of idolizing me, an attitude that reveals her latent disparagement even with regard to form, since idolizing is hardly a suitable attitude for a relationship with a Jew.

But the preoccupying element in the 'two-squares' dream is the police who divide the demonstrators—a police force that is strong enough to prevent conflict (and also the dominating factor in the scene) and strong enough also to justify the cynical attitude that allows them to agree with everything anyone says, like the head of department.

Here can be seen an element that seemed to me to be symptomatic in attributing a Jewish identity to me: the desired inconfrontability of differences—between sexes, generations, and cultures—signalling an emotive position of stalemate, which has been sought in order to confront the problem of what she has inherited from her forebears, including their guilt, a step that is necessary, as pointed out by Chasseguet-Smirgel (chapter three, this volume), in emancipation. If emancipation is not possible, only betrayal is possible, and the sado-masochistic relationship that can be set up between the tell-tale and her boss.

Another woman patient's dream is equally interesting. The dream was as follows:

> I am in a room, a large kitchen . . . there is a big wooden table . . . then there's a dog that comes up to me and puts his face on my open neckline. . . . I am very frightened and angry that no one—and there are a lot of people there—does anything to help me. Then I go out, I don't know if it's because I'm taking the dog out or because I'm being dragged by the dog, and then I come back in, but I notice that the room is changed. It's large, with beautiful windows open at the far end, with no curtains, there's a Jewish ceremony. . . . I feel there's danger around, I think they're rash to hold it like that, without even closing the curtains. I look out of the window, and sure enough, I can see people looking from the houses opposite. With the help of a friend I try to lower the roller shutters. Then I go downstairs and find myself in a large room, like a conference room, with a lot of people in it. Again, the feeling of danger. I find a colleague with papers from my office under his arm. I explain my fears to him, and he says this is true, but he doesn't seem to have any intention of changing the programme. Then I run away with a little girl . . . it's a hill town, and I'm running along a street downhill. There's a food shop, full of all kinds of things. While I'm asking about the bread—I had thought I would stop because the little girl was hungry—I look

outside and see a fire has broken out in the meantime. . . .
I realize I have to get away. I continue downhill and reach
a large building, where I think I'll have to ask for refuge. I
see that, near the doorbell of the people I'm looking for, is
our bell. I think it's impossible that you should be there
unperturbed. I go up the stairs and ask the owner if he
can take us in. He asks me to wait while he asks his wife. I
feel he is in great danger too, and I know I won't hold it
against him if he doesn't take me in. However, quite
unexpectedly, he tells me his wife agrees and he can take
us in . . . he'll put us in a little room with a secret door in
the wall. . . . I ask the little girl if she wants something to
eat, but she's so tired she just asks to be able to lie down.
At that moment I remember you and ask the owner what
has become of your family and you. . . . I feel great anxiety
and wake up suddenly.

In the associations, the fact comes out—very curiously—that, she says, I had never told her I was Jewish. In her opinion, this explains why she was so alarmed when she found herself involved in her dream in a Jewish ceremony. And if I had kept this from her, perhaps it was because I am afraid . . . however, in her dream she thinks I am rash . . . that I underestimate the danger. When she came to me, she was very much afraid of dogs, but now she isn't, and she thinks it is strange that they should re-appear in her dreams. There was certainly a strange atmosphere . . . if she hadn't woken up, perhaps she might have found out what had become of me.

I told her that evidently either her dream was finished, or my family and I were no more. . . . The patient said she felt she was very much on my side, she was sorry her dream was like that . . . she was ashamed of it . . . however, she was on my side in the dream too . . . and detached, too . . . on a parallel, yes, a parallel sort of destiny.

What have these two patients got in common? Why do both have to resort to Jews or Jewishness to portray and express otherwise inaccessible mental contents and feelings? The first patient is admittedly the daughter of a fascist, but certainly not of a war criminal: in fact, her father had even rescued a Jew. The second does not even have fascist traditions in her family.

And yet, if her dream had not come to an end, she would have had me come to a bad end.

Even in these fragments of analysis, as you can see, the question of the father takes a prominent position. Freud's hypothesis, later taken up by many other psychoanalysts, about antisemitism being indissolubly linked to the question of the father—and more specifically to the question of parricide—is a fundamental issue here too. But, as far as these antisemites are concerned—and given that we cannot put antisemitism itself on the couch, in the same way as we cannot put a convinced antisemite on the couch—we can see that their antisemitism admittedly sinks into the question of the father, but that it is expressed primarily through an image of unbridgeability through radical emphasis of the differences. These differences concern the question of guilt. 'They will not accept it as true that they murdered God, whereas we admit it and have been cleansed of that guilt' (Freud, 1939a [1937–39], p. 136]. This is the reproof that, according to Freud, the antisemites use against the Jews, because the Jews, so to speak, deserve to be persecuted.

But the father is also the law, the law that separates, distinguishes, that creates a space that is the very space of thought, in the same way as the order not to make any image of God means, on the one hand, 'that a sensory perception was given second place to what may be called an abstract idea' (p. 133) and therefore 'a triumph of intellectuality over sensuality' (p. 133) but also, more importantly, means distinguishing clearly between the realm of thought alone and those things pertaining also to the realm of feeling.

Both patients—in their own ways—put themselves on their fathers' sides: one, however, by fleeing from a persecution that smacks of seduction (the dog, the fire) but separating her destiny from mine through a renunciation of thought (the little girl's sleepiness, the womb-room); the other puts herself on my side as a *tell-tale* for my benefit, but also in order to atone for her father's guilt (in Italian there is a punning connection between *spia* [spy, tell-tale] and *espiare* [to atone for]): the relationship she offers me is a sado-masochistic one, which emphasizes the impossibility of a personal relationship on an equal basis.

But the problem is that the father, in the case of these two patients, stands for several contrasting things, each in its own right. And, especially in the first patient, one can even perceive at times a sense of irony in a situation that allows her always to be on the side of a father, but never to recognize one as hers. Even the opening phrase, 'I wonder what my father would have said . . .', can change a lot in meaning according to the tone in which it is said. This position enables one, in a certain sense, to agree with everything anyone says, to be tolerant. But this agreeing with everyone—with fascists and Jews alike, with Palestinians and Israelis—this recognizing them all as fathers, might this not be a desire to see the return of matriarchy, a longed-for triumph of polytheism, a return to sensitivity as against abstract representation?

'France or Spain, as long as we can eat', and 'Go, go, poor little plague-spreader, you won't be the one to ruin Milan' (A. Manzoni, *I Promessi Sposi* [*The Betrothed*], end of chap. 34), are perhaps, to return to our theme of everyday antisemitism, guiding principles that have become more and more valid in Italy: acceptance of everybody, because there is no longer any law anywhere, is only a sign of wanting nature—which is immortal, certainly, because it is unreflecting and non-individualized—to be superior to mortals, to the dead, and to humanity as we know it.

This humanity, felt to be something else, both desired and feared, considered to be something unattainable, is characterized by the tolerability of conflict and by the creative symbolic overcoming of generation differences in the identity of introjected parental functions. It is therefore relatively intolerant of what annuls, rather than breaks, the law. Hence this form of human organization is to be annulled rather than fought against, with a preference for a sort of omnipotent undifferentiation rather than differentiation that is limiting in any way.

And so there it is, in a nutshell. I only wonder whether this particular interpretation of antisemitism in the context of non-recognition of the law might not constitute a specific quality of Italian-style antisemitism, a quality that would then seem to be less reassuring than is sometimes held to be the case, not only for the destiny of the Jews—not exactly idyllic in Italy, although not as alarming as in other countries either, and as long as their numbers remain small, they will be tolerated like any other group—but because, if antisemitism is also the sign of western societies' profound inability to come to terms with themselves, this type of antisemitism, characterized by a desire to avoid conflict through a sort of multiplicity of guiding principles, may be the sign of a perverse form of evolution, where, I believe, in the long run will reappear the object of repression: a terrible, murdered primogenital father, a society where the struggle between brothers acknowledges force as the only criterion.

BIBLIOGRAPHY AND REFERENCES

AA.VV (1981). *La psychanalyse est elle une histoire juive?* Colloque de Montpellier, 1980 (edited by A. & J.-J. Rassial). Paris: Ed. de Seuil. [The symposium was held under the auspices of the French section of B'nai B'rith.]

——— (1989). Catalogue of exhibition, 'Italy in Psychoanalysis', held by Istituto dell'Enciclopedia Italiana, Rome (edited by Arnaldo Novelletto).

Arendt, H. (1958). *Rahel Varnhagen.* New York: Harcourt Brace Jovanovich.

——— (1966). *Between Past and Future.* Magnolia, MA: Peter Smith.

Arlow, J. A. (1951). The consecration of the prophet. *Psychoanalytic Quarterly,* 2: 374–397.

Baeck, L. (1905). *Das Wesen des Judentum.* [Italian edition, Genoa: Marietti, 1988.]

Bakan, D. (1958). *Sigmund Freud and the Jewish Mystical Tradition.* London: Free Association Books.

Beirnaert, L., Bori, P. C., Hassoun, J., & Winter, J. P. (1976). Studi su 'Mose e il Monoteismo'. *Sic, materiali per la psicoanalisi* (September–October).

Benjamin, W. (1927–40). *Das Passagen-Werk.* Frankfurt am Main: Surkamp Verlag, 1982.
Bettelheim, B. (1983). *Freud and Man's Soul.* London: Chatto & Windus.
Bloom, H. (1975). *Kabbalah and Criticism.* A Continuum Book. New York: Seabury Press
Bori, P. C. (1975). Materiale storico religioso nella biblioteca di S. Freud: alcuni rilievi sul catalogo. *Annali dell'Istituto storico-germanico in Trento* (pp. 281–289).
―――― (1979). 'Avvertenza editoriale' and 'L'Uomo Mosè e la religione monoteistica.' In: *S. Freud, Opere, Vol. 11.* Turin: Boringhieri.
―――― (1979). Una pagina inedita di Freud: la premessa del romanzo storico su Mosè. *Rivista di storia contemporanea, 1*: 1–17.
Brill, A. A., & Kuttner, A. (Trans.) (1918). *Reflections on 'War and Death', by S. Freud.* New York: Moffat, Yard.
Cacciari, M. (1985). Dalla bocca di Mosè. In: *Icone della legge* (pp. 138–152). Milan: Adelphi.
Canestri, J. (1985). Allegoria con giardino: di quel che intercorre tra la psicoanalisi, le scienze, l'arte. Review, in *Il Piccolo Hans*, no. 46 (April–June), pp. 45–59.
―――― (1986). La fantasia scientifica. Una nota di lettura sulla 'Sintesi delle nevrosi di traslazione' di S. Freud. *Rivista di Psicoanalisi, 32* (4) (October–November): 591–602.
―――― (1988). La risonanza e lo scarto. Review, in *Il Piccolo Hans*, no. 60.
Castagnoli Manghi, A., & Terracini, L. (1982). Le invarianti e le variabili dell'inganno, Don Juan Manuel, Cervantes, Andersen, il re nudo. In: *L'immagine riflessa. Semestrale di sociologia dei testi letterari.* Genoa: Casa editrice Tilgher.
Celan, P. (1963). *La rose de personne* (translated by M. Broda). Paris: Nouveau Commerce, 1977.
Certeau, M. De (1975). *L'écriture de l'histoire.* Paris: Gallimard.
Chasseguet-Smirgel, J. (1973). *The Ego Ideal.* London: Free Association Books.
―――― (1984). The archaic matrix of the Oedipus complex. In: *Sexuality and Mind.* New York: New York University Press, 1986. [Reprinted London: Karnac Books, 1989.]
―――― (1985). The paradox of the Freudian Method. In: *Sexuality*

and Mind. New York: New York University Press, 1986. [Reprinted London: Karnac Books, 1989.]
———— (1986). Nous agitons la chevelure blanche du temps: réflexions sur le Congrès de Hambourg, 1985. *Revue Française de Psychanalyse, 50* (3): 1021–1032.
Chasseguet-Smirgel, J., & Grünberger, B. (1979). *Freud or Reich?* London: Free Association Books.
Devoto, G., & Oli, G. C. (1975). *Dizionario della lingua italiana.* Florence: Le Monnier.
Epstein, I. (1959). *Judaism.* New York: Pelican Books.
Ey, H. (1952). *Etudes psychiatriques, Vol. 1.* Paris: Desclée de Brouwer.
Fenichel, O. (1937). The scoptophilic instinct and identification. *International Journal of Psycho-Analysis, 18*: 6–34.
Freud, E. (Ed.) (1960). *Letters of Sigmund Freud.* New York: Basic Books.
———— (Ed.) (1970). *The Letters of Sigmund Freud and Arnold Zweig* (translated by E. & W. D. Robbson-Scott). London: The Hogarth Press & The Institute of Psycho-Analysis; New York: Harcourt Brace & World.
Freud, S. (1882), Letter to Martha, 26 August. In: E. Jones, *Sigmund Freud: Life and Works, Vol. 1* (p. 191). London, Hogarth Press, 1980.
———— (1898b). The psychical mechanism of forgetfulness. *S.E., 3.*
———— (1900a). *The Interpretation of Dreams. S.E., 4–5.*
———— (1901b). *The Psychopathology of Everyday Life. S.E., 6.*
———— (1905c). *Jokes and their Relation to the Unconscious. S.E., 8.*
———— (1907–26). *A Psycho-Analytic Dialogue: The Letters of Sigmund Freud and Karl Abraham* (edited by H. C. Abraham and E. L. Freud; translated by B. Marsh & H. C. Abraham). London: Hogarth Press, 1965.
———— (1909–1939). *Psychoanalysis and Faith: The Letters of Sigmund Freud and Oscar Pfister* (edited by H. Meng and E. L. Freud). London: Hogarth Press & the Institute of Psycho-Analysis, 1963.
———— (1909d). Notes upon a case of obsessional neurosis. *S.E., 10.*
———— (1911b). Formulations on the Two Principles of Mental Functioning. *S.E., 12.*
———— (1912–13). *Totem and Taboo. S.E., 13.*

_____ (1912–1936). *Sigmund Freud and Lou Andreas-Salomé: Letters* (edited by E. Pfeiffer). London: Hogarth Press & The Institute of Psycho-Analysis, 1972.
_____ (1915). *A Phylogenetic Phantasy: Overview of the Transference Neuroses* (edited by I. Grubrich-Simitis). Cambridge, MA: Harvard University Press.
_____ (1915b). Thoughts for the times on war and death. *S.E.*, 14, 275–300.
_____ (1916a). On transience. *S.E.*, 14.
_____ (1916–17). *Introductory Lectures on Psycho-Analysis. S.E.*, 15–16.
_____ (1917e [1915]). Mourning and melancholia, *S.E.*, 14.
_____ (1918b [1914]). From the history of an infantile neurosis, *S.E.*, 17.
_____ (1919h). The 'uncanny'. *S.E.*, 17.
_____ (1921c). *Group Psychology and the Analysis of the Ego. S.E.*, 18.
_____ (1925b). Letter to the Editor of the *Jüdische Presszentrale*, Zurich. *S.E.*, 19.
_____ (1925d [1924]). *An Autobiographical Study. S.E.*, 20.
_____ (1925e [1924]). The resistances to psycho-analysis. *S.E.*, 19.
_____ (1926d [1925]). *Inhibitions, Symptoms and Anxiety. S.E.*, 20.
_____ (1927d). Humour. *S.E.*, 21.
_____ (1930a). *Civilization and its Discontents. S.E.*, 21.
_____ (1931b). Female sexuality. *S.E.*, 21.
_____ (1933a). *New Introductory Lectures on Psycho-Analysis. S.E.*, 22.
_____ (1934). Quoted in Y. H. Yerushalmi, *Freud's Moses. Judaism Terminable and Interminable*. New Haven, CT/London: Yale University Press, 1991.
_____ (1934b [1930]). Preface to the Hebrew Translation of *Totem and Taboo. S.E.*, 13.
_____ (1935a). Postscript (1935) to *An Autobiographical Study. S.E.*, 20.
_____ (1935c). Thomas Mann on his Sixtieth Birthday. *S.E.*, 22.
_____ (1937d). Constructions in Analysis. *S.E.*, 23.
_____ (1938c). Letter to the Editor of *Time and Tide*, Nov. 26, 1938, p. 1649; 'Anti-Semitism in England'. *S.E.*, 23.

_____ (1939a [1937–39]). *Moses and Monotheism. S.E.*, 23.
_____ (1940a [1938]). *An Outline of Psycho-Analysis. S.E.*, 23.
_____ (1941e [1926]). Address to the Members of the B'nai B'rith. *S.E.*, 20.
_____ (1970). *The Letters of Sigmund Freud and Arnold Zweig* (edited by E. L. Freud; translated by E. & W. D. Robbson-Scott). London: The Hogarth Press & The Institute of Psycho-Analysis: New York: Harcourt Brace & World.
_____ (1985). *The Complete Letters of Sigmund Freud to Wilhelm Fliess (1887–1904)*. Cambridge: The Belknap Press of Harvard University Press.
Gay, P. (1979). *Freud, Jews and Other Germans*. London/New York: Oxford University Press.
_____ (1987). *A Godless Jew*. New Haven, CT: Yale University Press.
_____ (1988). *Freud. A Life for Our Time*. New York/London: W. W. Norton.
Giniewski, P. (1978). *Simone Weil ou la haine de soi*, Paris: Berg International.
Ginzberg, L. (1909–38). *The Legend of the Jews*. Philadelphia.
Ginzburg, C. (1986). *Miti, emblemi, spie (morfologie e storia)*. Turin: Einaudi.
Giorello, G. (1976). Introduction. In: I. Lakatos, *Proofs and Refutations: The Logic of Mathematical Discovery*. Cambridge: Cambridge University Press. Italian edition: Milan, Feltrinelli.
Heine, H. (1982). *The Complete Poems of Heinrich Heine: A Modern English Version* (translated by Hal Draper). Boston: Surkamp/Insel.
Herzl, T. (1896). *The Jewish State*. New York: Dover, 1989.
Jones, E. (1953–57). *Sigmund Freud: Life and Work, Vols. 1–3*. London: Hogarth Press.
Jung, C. G. (1934). The state of psychotherapy today. In: *Collected Works, Vol. 10: Civilization in Transition*. Princeton, NJ: Princeton University Press.
_____ (1952). Answer to Job. In: *Collected Works, Vol. 9: Psychology and Religion*. London: Routledge.
Kafka, F. (1902–24). *Briefe*. Frankfurt am Main: Fischer Verlag, 1958.
Klein, D. B. (1981). *Jewish Origins of the Psychoanalytic Movement*. Chicago, IL/London: University of Chicago Press, 1985.

Lakatos, I. (1976). *Proofs and Refutations: The Logic of Mathematical Discovery.* Cambridge: Cambridge University Press.

Laqueur, W. (1972). *A History of Zionism.* London

Levi, P. (1947). *If This Is a Man.* London: Orion Press, 1960.

Magris, C. (1967). *Lontano da dove. Joseph Roth e la tradizione ebraico orientale.* Torino: Einaudi.

Marx, K. (1843). Zur Judenfrage. In: *Werke, Vol. 1.* Berlin: Dietz Verlag, 1961.

_____ (1844). *A propos de la question juive.* Paris: Aubier-Montaigne, 1971.

Masson, J. M. (Transl. & Ed.) (1985). *The Complete Letters of Sigmund Freud to Wilhelm Fliess, 1887–1904.* Cambridge, MA/London: Harvard University Press & Belknap Press.

Mayne, E. (Trans.) (1925). 'Thoughts for the times on war and death' by S. Freud. In *Collected Papers, Vol. 4* (pp. 288–317). London: Hogarth & The Institute of Psycho-Analysis.

Meghnagi, D. (1985a). Freud e l'immaginazione ebraica. In *Modelli freudiani della critica e teoria psicoanalitica* (pp. 89–100). Rome: Bulzoni.

_____ (1985b). Una societa di 'paria' e di 'luftmenshn'. Gli ebrei dell'Est, il socialismo ebraico, la questione ebraica. Considerazioni storico-psicologiche. In: AA.VV., *Gli ebrei dell'Europa orientale dall'utopia alla rivolta: 1897–1943.* Milano: Ediz. Di Comunita.

_____ (1986). Il ritorno del rimosso: Freud e il mito ebraico. In: AA.VV., *Psicoanalisi e narrazione* (pp. 145–154). Ancona: Il Lavoro editoriale.

_____ (Ed.) (1987a). *L'altra scena della psicoanalisi. Tensioni ebraiche nell'opera di Sigmund Freud.* Roma: Carucci editore.

_____ (1987b). 'The dancer balancing on the tip of one toe' and 'Freud and "The man Moses"'. *Annali di storia dell'esegesi*, 7 (1), 1990: 311–321.

_____ (1987c). Freud e il mito ebraico. In: AA.VV (E. Morpurgo & V. Egidi, Eds.), *Psicoanalisi e narrazione* (pp. 145–154). Ancona: Il Lavoro Editoriale.

_____ (1988). Primo Levi e la scrittura. In: *Lettera Internazionale*, 21: 18–20. Rome: Edit. Lettera Internazionale

_____ (1989a). Le figure dell'ebreo e dell'antisemita nello humour ebraico. In: AA.VV. *Ebraismo e antiebraismo: immagine e pregiudizio* (pp. 1–9). Florence: La Giuntina.

‎ ‎ ‎ ‎ ‎ ‎ (1989b). Freud e la coscienza ebraica contemporanea. In AA.VV. (D. Bidussa, Ed.), *Ebrei moderni* (pp. 96–112). Turin: Bollati Boringhieri.

‎ ‎ ‎ ‎ ‎ ‎ (Ed.) (1989c). *Studi freudiani* (pp. 85–95). Milan: Guerini.

‎ ‎ ‎ ‎ ‎ ‎ (1991). Jewish humour on psychoanalysis. *International Review of Psycho-Analysis, 15* (2): 223–228.

Meltzer, D. (1986). *Studies in Extended Metapsychology.* The Roland Harris Education Trust. Strathclyde: Clunie Press.

Meyer-Palmedo, I., & Fichtner, G. (1989). *Freud-Bibliographie mit Werkkonkordanz.* Frankfurt am Main: S. Fischer Verlag.

Mosse, G. L. (1985). *German Jews beyond Judaism.* Bloomington, IN: Indiana University Press.

Musatti, C. (1957). *Trattato di Psicoanalisi.* Turin: Edizioni Scientifiche Einaudi. [Turin: Boringhieri, 1967.]

‎ ‎ ‎ ‎ ‎ ‎ (1982). 'Freud e l'ebraismo' and 'L'umorismo come vocazione ebraica e l'opera di Woody Allen'. In: *Mia sorella gemella la psicoanalis.* Roma: Editori Riuniti.

Nitzschke, B. (1990). Wir und der Tod. Ein Stück wiedergefundener Geistes-Geschichte. *Die Zeit, 30* (20 July).

Nunberg, H. (1961). Curiosity. In: *Practice and Theory of Psychoanalysis, Vol. 2.* New York: International Universities Press.

Ostow, M. (1982). *Judaism and Psychoanalysis.* New York: Ktav Publishing House.

‎ ‎ ‎ ‎ ‎ ‎ (1986) Archetypes of apocalypse in dreams, fantasies and in religious scripture. *Israel Journal of Psychiatry and Related Sciences, 23* (2): 107–122 [also in *American Imago 43* (4): 307–334; *Conservative Judaism 39,* 4: 42–55 (Summer, 1987)].

Pfeiffer, E. (Ed.) (1972). *Sigmund Freud and Lou Andreas-Salomé: Letters.* London: The Hogarth Press & The Institute of Psycho-Analysis.

Poliakov, L. (1973). *The Arian Myth: A History of Racist and Nationalistic Ideas in Europe.* New York: NAL-Dutton, 1977.

Popper, K. (1934).*The Logic of Scientific Discovery.* London: Hutchinson.

Reichenbach, H. (1935). Two notes on induction and demarcation. Discussion on a study of Reichenbach's presented in Prague in 1934. *Erkenntniss, 5.*

Reik, T. (1929). Zur Psychoanalyse des jüdischen Witzes. *Imago, 15:* 63–88.

‎ ‎ ‎ ‎ ‎ ‎ (1954). Freud and Jewish wit. *Psychoanalysis, 21:* 12–20.

―――― (1962). *Jewish Wit*. New York: Gamut Press.
Richards, A. (1974) Freud bibliography. In: *S.E.*, 24: 47-82. London: Hogarth Press & The Institute of Psycho-Analysis.
Robert, M. (1974). *From Oedipus to Moses: Freud's Jewish Identity*. Garden City, NY: Anchor Books.
Rossi, S. (1983). *Teresa d'Avila, biografia di una scrittrice*. Rome: Editori Riuniti.
―――― (1987). *Ascoltare Cervantes, saggio biografico*. Rome: Editori Riuinti.
Rothman, S. & Isenberg, P. (1974). Freud and Jewish marginality. *Encounter*: 46–54.
Rubinstein, R. (1958). *The Religious Imagination: A Study in Psychoanalysis and Jewish Theology*. New York: Bobbs-Merrill. [Reprinted Maryland: University Press of America, 1985.]
―――― (1968). *L'immaginazione religiosa. Studio sulla psicoanalisi e la teologia ebraica*. Rome: Ubaldini Editore, 1974.
Rürup, R. (1975). Emancipation und Antisemitismus. In: *Kritische Studien zur Geschichtswissenschaft, Vol. 15*. Göttingen: Vandenshoeck & Ruprecht.
Sacerdoti, G. (1987). Ebraismo e psicoanalisi davanti all'assimilazione. In: D. Meghangi (Ed.), *L'altra scena della psicoanalisi* (pp. 29–53). Roma: Carucci.
―――― (1988a). *Irony through Psychoanalysis*. London: Karnac Books, 1992.
―――― (1988b). Problemi di applicazione e sviluppo della psicoanalisi. In: A. Semi. (Ed.), *Trattato di psicoanalisi, Vol. 2*. Milano: Raffaello Cortina, 1989–90.
Sachar, A. L. (1964). *A History of the Jews*, New York: Alfred A. Knopf.
Sartre, J. P. (1954). *Antisemite and Jew*. New York: Schocken Books, 1968.
Schlesinger, K. (1973). Jewish humour and Jewish identity. *International Review of Psycho-Analysis*, 6: 317–330.
Scholem, G. (1957). *Die jüdische Mystik in ihren Hauptströmungen*. English edition: New York: Schocken Books, 1954.
Strachey, J. (1957). Editorial note to 'Thoughts for the times on war and death'. In: *S.E.*, 14: 274. London: Hogarth Press & The Institute of Psycho-Analysis.
Vermorel, H., & Vermorel, M. (1986). Was Freud a Romantic? *International Journal of Psycho-Analysis*, 13, 1: 15–37.

Weininger, O. (1903). *Sex and Character.* New York: AMS Press.
Yerushalmi, Y. H. (1982). *Zakhor, Jewish History and Jewish Memory.* Philadelphia: Jewish Publication Society; Seattle & London: University of Washington Press.
Zweimonats-Bericht für die Mitglieder der österr. israel. Humanitätsvereine B'nai B'rith, 18 (1): 41–51.

INDEX

Abraham, K., 5, 47, 60, 85
Abraham, 83
Achilles, 26
Adler, A., 50
aggression, xvi
agrarian society, separation from, 97
alcoholism, 143
Allen, W., 99
Andersen, H. C., 61
Angleichung [assimilation], 135
'Annie Hall', 113
antisemitism:
    egosyntonic, 145
    fear of, 109
    fight against, 74
    films denouncing, 105
    first use of word, 80
    and Freud, 65
        attitude of to Judaism, 85
    and Jewish psychosis, 83
    'Moses' as scientific response to, 121
    in German-speaking area, 76
    Italian, 142, 143, 150
    and Jewish assimilation, 80
    need to confront, 42
    as non-recognition of law, 150
    psychoanalysis as victim of, 60
    psychoanalysis in response to, 58
    psychopathology of, 141
    of Rahel Varnhagen, 78
    right-wing, 73
    and theme of the father, 149
Anzengruber, L., 31, 32
API Congress, Hamburg, 90

apocalypse, xvii
Arendt, H., 61, 65, 70, 78, 79, 80
Argives, 26
Arlow, J. A., xxi
Ashkenazim, 106
Asra, 15
assimilation, of Jews, xxiv, xxvii
  dynamics of, 135
  in Europe, 68
  history of, 76–85
  in nineteenth century, 79
  introjective, 137
  projective, 135, 137
  psychoanalysis in answer to, 57
  and religious reform, 85
  spontaneous, 138
  success of, 80
  between World Wars, 83
Atkinson, 22

Babel, I. E., 73
Baeck, L., 45
Bakan, D., 121
Balfour, A. J., 48
  declaration, 47
Balzac, H. de, 35
barbarity and progress, 124
Bauer, B., 80
Benjamin, W., 64
Bergman, M., 89
Bettelheim, B., 30
Bildung, 42, 64, 65, 75
Binswanger, L., 43
Bion, W., 67
Blatt, S., xxix
B'nai B'rith, xxiii
  lecture to, 3–9, 41–53
Boehm, F., 90
Bonaparte, M., 89

Book of Revelation, xvii
Bori, P. C., 44
Boveda, X., 89
Brill, A. A., 6
Broszat, M., 88
Buber, M., 58
Bund, 84
  rise of, 58
  vs. Zionists, 59

Canestri, J., xxiv, xxviii, xxix, 117–129
Canetti, E., 97
Cassirer, E., 69
Castagnoli Manghi, A., 62
causality, need for, xxiii
Celan, P., 92
Cervantes, M., 62
Chaplin, C., 105, 111
Chasseguet-Smirgel, J., xxiv, xxvii, xxix, 73–92, 137, 147
Chassidic Jewish stories, 111
Cicero, 126
civilization, 29, 30, 38
  discontents in, and psychoanalysis, 98
  dynamism of, xxviii
  as elite minority, 102
  Freud's writings on, 66
  and prohibition of incest, 101
  technological, 96
  western, assimilation of Jewish culture of, 100
communication:
  humouristic, 104
  relationships of, 97
communism:
  and Freud, 84
  as solution against antisemitism, 84

INDEX

competitive spirit, 97
conflict, internalization of, and psychoanalysis, 96
constructs, exemplifying, 118
conversion, in Jewish world, xxiv, 63, 80
    escape through, 61
    movement of, 78
    religious, 138
Corrao, F., xxix
'Crossfire', 105
curiosity:
    of animate organisms, xvi
    of children, xix
    gratification of, and identification, xxi
    and illusions, xxii
    and knowledge, xvi
    pathologic, xviii
    and psychoanalysis, xv–xxv
    and psychoanalytic method, xix
    religious, xvii

Darwin, C., 22
death:
    denial of, 36
    fear of, 28
    and Jews, 11–39
    life after, 25, 45
    and primaeval man, 20–28
    and unconscious, 31
    -wish, 36
defence:
    mechanisms, 98
    metapsychological, from archaic anxieties, 104
deforming tendencies [*entstellenden Tendenzen*], 117
Denkarbeit [workings of thought], 122

Denkprozess [thought process], 123
deprecation, cultural self-, 52
Descartes, R., 126
Devoto, G., 138
Diaspora, xxv, 77, 84
    Sephardite, 63
'Dictator, The', 111
Draco, Athenian code of, 33
Dreyfus, A., 105
    affair, 42, 58, 84
Duke of Naxos, 63
Durkheim, E., 69

ego ideal, corruption and degradation of, 124
Einstein, A., 58, 69
elaboration:
    lack of, 100
    literary, 118, 128
    missing, 100
    psychoanalytic, 69
    re-, technical, 96
    scientific, 118, 128
Enlightenment, the, 76, 77, 80
    culture of, 134
    effect of, on European Jews, 78
    humanism of, 78
enlightenment, 64, 66
    logic of, 125
entstellenden Tendenzen [deforming tendencies], 117
epistemology, 117, 118, 119
Epstein, I., 85
erotism, childhood, xix
essence of Jewishness, 126
ethics, and Jews, 95–102
ex-hodos [Exodus], 127
exegesis, xvi
Exodus, 127

INDEX

Ezekiel, xix, xx

Fachinelli, E., xxix
Falstaff, 12
fantasy, xv, xxiii, 113
   phylogenetic, 136
   and reasoning, 128
   scientific, 127
fascism, effects of, 143
father, 142, 149, 150
   and antisemitism, 149
   authoritarian, 99
   complex, 59
   guilt of, 149
   Jewish, 59
   Jewishness of, 66
   and law, 149
   murderous instinct towards, 66
   primal, killing of, 22, 23, 151
   relationship with, 66
   –son relationship, 97
   turning to, and abandoning mother, 122
Faust, 65
Fenichel, O., xxi
Ferenczi, S., 44, 128
Fichtner, G., 4
figuration, concept of, 117
Fiktion [fiction], 122
Finzi, S. V., xxviii, xxix, 95–102
Fliess, W., 58, 63, 81
France, A., 44
Frankfurt School, 67, 69
Franz Joseph, Emperor, 41
Frazer, J. G., 31
free association, based on Jewish method of scripture study, 62
French Revolution, 58
Freud, Alexander, 42

Freud, Anna, 121
Freud, E., 51, 86, 89, 92
Freud, J., 97, 98
Freud, M., 47
Freud, S., xviii, xxii, xxix, 3–9, 11–39
   on analysis and civilization, xxviii
   on antisemitism, 141
   and Benjamin, link between work of, 64
   on Church, 49
   on civilization, xxiv, xxviii, 66
   on civilized behaviour, xxiv
   on comedy, 105, 106
   and communism, 84
   correspondence with Zweig, 86–87
   on crowd, 49
   culture of, Jewish side of, 86
   education of, 86
   epistemology of, 117
   Germanic background of, and Nazism, 85–92
   on humour, 105–107, 108
   on identification, 135
   identification of with Hannibal, 142
   Jewish creativeness of, 66
   Jewish element in works of, xxvii, 74–75, 77, 84, 124
   on Jewish humour, 104
   Jewish heritage of, xxviii, 46, 49, 60, 74–75, 76, 86, 138
      ambivalence towards, 84
      reflections of on, 101
   and Jewish identity, 67, 83
   Jewish self-perception of, 69

INDEX 167

Freud, S. *(contd.)*
 on Jewish witticism, 103
 on Judaism, xxviii, 134
 and Kafka, link between work of, 60, 64
 letter to Thomas Mann, 89
 literary significance of, 60
 on nakedness, 61
 on nature of Judaism, xxiii
 and Nazism, 73–92
 on science and on Judaism, xxviii
 relationship of to Jewishness, 60
 and religious conversion, 138
 research of, logic of, 117–129
 scientific thinking of, bound up with Jewishness, 66
 self-analysis of, 126, 129, 142
 on truth, 68
 on wit, 105, 106
 on World War I, 47
 Zionist sympathies of, 86
Friedländer, D., 78
Funari, E., xxix
future, wish to know, xv

Garden of Eden, xxi
Gay, P., xxvii, 45, 47, 48, 50, 51, 60, 120, 127
Geiger, A., 85
Geistigkeit [intellectuality], 122
'Gentlemen's Agreement', 105
German–Jewish symbiosis, 67
German–Jewish synthesis, 64
ghettos:
 humour of, 105, 110
 opening of, 58, 59, 62, 63

Giniewski, P., 82, 83
Giorello, G., 119
Gleichschaltung, 85, 88
Goethe, J. W. von, 75, 86
 Associations, 75
golem, legend of, xxiii
Grottenauer, 80
Grünberger, B., 88, 137
Grynspan, 88
guilt:
 blood-, 29
 conversion as cause of, 61
 primal, 22–23

Habermas, J., 88
Hacham, 110
Hagigah, xxii, xxiii
Hamlet, 4, 44
Hammurabi, code of, 43
Hannibal, 136, 142
Hans the Stone-Breaker, 31
Hanseatic League, 16
Hautmann, G., xxix
Hebrew, abandonment of, 85
Hebrew University of Jerusalem, xxix, 48
Hegel, G. W. F., 82
Heine, H., 15, 26, 27, 52, 64, 77, 79
Heiß, S., 3
Heller, H., 5
heresies, in Jewish world, 63
Herzl, T., 42, 58, 84
heuristics, 118, 119, 128
historiography, Jewish, xxv
Hitler, A., 50, 87, 88, 89, 104
Hitschmann, E., 42
Holdheim, S., 85
Homer, 26
human race, universality of, 100

humour, Jewish, xxiv, 103, 104, 108, 109, 110, 111, 112, 113
   cinematographic, 109–110
   jokes, 45, 46
      cynical, 35
   literary, 109–110
   tragic and dramatic aspects of, 108
   types of, 105
   as vocation, 103–113

identity, Jewish, see Jewish identity
idolatry, rejection of, 45, 77
ignorance, effects of, xvi
immortality, belief in, 28, 31
impulse:
   hostile, 8
   unconscious, 8
incest, prohibition of, 100
Innsbruck International Congress, 105
Institute for Social Research, 67
intellectuality:
   [*Geistigkeit*], 122
   and detachment from matter, 122
   progress of, 123, 124, 127
   triumph of over sensuality, 149
intellectuals and Jews, convergence of, 101
International Psychoanalytical Association, 60, 96
International Psychoanalytical Conference, Paris, 121
introjection, 66
   scoptophilic, and wish to become God, xxi

introjective identification, 135
Isaiah, 27, 68
Isenberg, P., 133, 138
Italian Psychoanalytical Society, xxix

Jäckel, E., 88
Jewish assimilation, see assimilation
Jewish consciousness, 48
   historical evolution of, 69
Jewish cultural ethos, 104
Jewish element in works of Freud, see Freud, S.
Jewish emancipation, 78
Jewish essence
   Freud's, 125
   mystery of, 124
Jewish historiography, xxv
Jewish humour, see humour, Jewish
Jewish identity, 58
   ambivalence regarding, 84
   assertion of, 83
   assimilated by western experience, 100
   crushing of, 84
   denial of, 83
   as elite minority, 101
   Freud's, see Freud, S.
   German, 75
   historical problem of, 66
   identified with modern society, 97
Jewish mysticism, 64
Jewish religion, xxiv, 77, 80, 81
   opposition to, 80
   as religion of reason, 74
   as religion without myth, 45
   struggle to maintain, 83
Jewish *Selbsthass*, 52

Jewish state in Palestine,
    restoration of, 85
Jews
    and Army, 50
    and Church, 50
    communicative skills of, 97
    and death, 11–39
    destiny of, xxiv
        concern with, and
            psychoanalysis, xxii
    entry of, into European
        culture, 79
    and ethics, 46, 95–102
    extermination of, 74
    and forced conversions,
        xxviii
    hostility towards, 74
    and intellectuals,
        convergence of, 101
    life of, xxii
    in modern society, xxvii
    origins of, xxii
    and religious texts, xvii
    response of to civilization,
        xxiv
Jofie, 87
Jones, E., 4, 5, 43, 45, 48, 50,
    85, 86, 87, 89, 104
Judaism:
    and literature, 62
    biblical, xvii
    and capitalism, 74
    and Christianity, opposition
        between, 100
    and civilized man, 46
    and communism, 74
    contemporary, history of,
        xxvii
    and democracy, 74
    foundation myth of, xxiii
    German-speaking, position
        of, 52

heresies of, xxviii
history of, xxviii
and humour, 103–113
    see also humour
in humanitarian
    representation, 46
and modernity, 74
nature of, Freud's
    excursions into, xxiv
    see also Freud, S.
and obscure memories of
    mankind, 46
pre-history of, xxiii
and psychoanalysis, 57–70
    see also psychoanalysis
rabbinical, xvii
religious vs. nationalistic
    aspects, 85
and socialism, 74
symbols of, abandoning, 85
teaching of, xxii
weakening of, by
    Enlightenment, 78
western, 47
in world religions, 45
Jung, C. G., 43, 44, 60, 67
    and Freud, 96

Kabbalist mystics, 63
Kafka, F., xxix, 58, 59, 63, 64,
    75
    and Freud, link between
        work of, 60
    Jewishness of, 60, 61
    literary significance of, 60,
        61
    on nakedness, 61
    on psychoanalysis, 57
Kaplan-Solms, K., 3
Klein, D. B., 4, 5, 6, 41, 42, 46
knowledge, instrumental value
    of, xvi

Königstein, L., 42
Kristallnacht, 88
Kuttner, A., 6

Lacan, J., 98
Lacoue-Labarthe, P., 124
Lakatos, I., 118, 119, 128, 129
Lamarck, J., xxviii, 68
Lampl-de-Groot, J., 90
language, development of, 122
Lessing, D., 78
Levi, G., xxix
Levi, P., 146
literature:
    Central European, 67
    fascist, 91
    and Judaism, 62
Little Hans, 81
logic of justification, 119
Lueger, K., 41

magic, xvi, xxiii
    search for, and mental illness, xviii
Magris, C., 110
'Manhattan', 112
Mann, T., 89
Manzoni, A., 150
marginality, ways of escape from, 133
Marr, W., 80
Marx, K., 82, 97
    anti-Jewish code of, 62
    Jewishness of, 80
    Selbsthass of, 80
Marxism, 80
Masson, J. M., 63
mathematics, xvii
Mayne, E., 6
Meghnagi, D., xxiii, xxiv, xxv, xxvii–xxix, 3, 4, 41–53, 57–70, 104, 121, 124

Meghnagi, M., xxix
Meltzer, D., 138
Mendelssohn, M., 78
Mersenne, M., 126
metapsychology, 101, 138
    witch of, xxiii
Meyer-Palmedo, I., 3, 4
Midrash Haggadah, 62
Mishnah, xvi
mobility, territorial, 97
modernity, hatred of, 74
Moebius, A. F., 43
Molko, 63
money-making, open-minded attitude towards, 97
monotheism, 44, 45, 86, 115
Montaigne, M. de, 62
morality, based on honour, 98
Morpurgo, E., xxix
Moses, xxii, xxiii, xxiv, xxviii, xxix, 13, 43, 44, 51, 52, 69, 115, 134, 136
    the Egyptian, 46, 100
    vs. Oedipus, the Greek, 126
    Freud's essays on, 66, 68
    and Jewish character, 51
Mosse, G. L., 74
mother, 91
    abandoning, and turning to father, 122
    Jewish, 99
    and needs of fetus, 91
    scheming, 99
mourning:
    work of, 51
    working-out of, 100
Munni, P., 105
Murray, A. T., 27
Musatti, C., xxiv, xxvii, xxix, 103–113

myth, xvii, xxv, xxviii, 101, 117, 120
  Cassirer's study of, 69
  Freudian, 66
  group, xxii
  and need for causality, xxiii
  origin, 100
  scientific, 127

nakedness:
  Freud on, 61
  Kafka on, 61
  as theme, historical origins of, 61
Nancy, J. L., 124
Napoleon Bonaparte, 78
National Socialist Party, 85
Nazism, 50, 51, 64, 68, 101
  and Freud, 73–92
neurosis, 36
  Woody Allen's, 113
'New York Stories', 99
Nipperdey, T., 88
Nolte, E., 88
Noue, J. Sauve de la, 53
Nunberg, H., xix, xxi
Nuremberg Laws, 91

Odysseus, 26
Oedipus, xxix, 58, 127
  complex, 126
    and Jewish monotheism, 86
  the Greek, vs. Moses, the Egyptian, 126
  problems, 141
Oli, G. C., 138
Ostow, M., xv-xxv, 3, 89

paganism:
  German, 90
  renunciation of, 77
Palestine, 85, 86, 87
paranoia, mechanisms of, Freud's discovery of, 68
parricide, 23, 141
  and antisemitism, 149
  primal crime of mankind, 22
patricide:
  archaic
    of primordial father, xxiii
  in pre-history of Judaism, xxiii
  and residue of guilt, xxiii
Pfeiffer, E., 47
pleasure principle, xxiv, 122
pogrom, 49
Poliakov, L., 96
Popper, K., 69, 118, 119, 128
Prince Hal, 12
progress, and barbarity, 124
projective identification, 135
proof control procedures, 119
prophecy, xvi
proselytism, dynamics of, 136
psychoanalysis:
  applied, xv, 138
  assimilation and proselytism, 133
  and curiosity, xv-xxv
  and discontents in civilization, 98
  ethics of, 126
  ethics of research in, 126
  and internalization of conflict, 96
  and Jewish experience, 57–70, 96, 113
  as Jewish joke, 66
  as Jewish story, xxix
  and methods of scripture study, 63

psychoanalysis *(contd.)*
   and morality, 46
   and origin myth, 100
   vs. other sciences, 63
   as response to Jewish situation in Europe, xxiv
   and revelation, xv–xxv
   as rooted in Jewish culture, 95
   rooted in minority culture, 102
   as science, xviii, xxiii, xxv, 60, 69
     and method, 97
     of unconscious, 101
   as source of salvation, xxiii
   unconscious does not exist outside, 98
   as under-water psychology, 8, 31
   universalization of, 86
   and Viennese Jewish culture, 96
   in Woody Allen's films, 113
psychologism, elimination of, 118

racism, 113
   antisemitic, xxviii
   Freud's Moses as scientific response to, 121
Rank, O., 45
Rashi, 57, 59
Rat Man, 44
Realität [reality], 122
reality principle, xxiv, 122
rebirth, xvi, xvii, xix
   hope for, xxi
   wish for, xv
Reformed Jewish Community, Berlin, 45

Reichenbach, H., 118
Reik, T., 104
reincarnation, 27
religion, xvii, xxii, xxiii, xxiv, 74, 98
   Jewish:
     adherence to, 77
     and dignity, 77
     and Freud, 124
     and self-esteem, 77
   Mosaic, 123
   myths of, xxiii
   reassurance against fear, xvi
   secret, of converts, 61
   theory of, 123
resistance, in dialogue, 68
Reubeni, 63
revelation, xv, xvi, xvii
   and psychoanalysis, xv–xxv
Richards, A., 4
Rie, O., 42
Rilke, R. M., 50
Robert, M., 121
Roman Gate in Siena, Freud's dream of, 59
Rossi, S., 62
Roth, J., 110
Rothman, S., 133, 138
Rousseau, J. J., 34, 35
Rozenzweig, 58
Rubinstein, R. L., 121
Rürup, R., 80

Sabbatianism, 63
Sacerdoti, G., xxvii, xxix, 104, 133–139, 138
Sachar, A. L., 78, 80
Saint-Exupéry, A. de, 110
Salomé, L., 47
Sandler, J., xxix
Sartre, J. P., 144
Scalpelli, S., xxix

INDEX

Schadchen, 110
Schlesinger, K., 109
Schnorrer, 110
Schoenberg, A. F. W., 58, 69
Scholem, G., xxviii, 64, 67
Schreber, D. G. M., 67, 68
Schulze, H., 88
science, xvii, 63, 101, 123
   and heuristics, 119
   of psychoanalysis, 97
   psychoanalysis as, 60, 69
scientific creativity,
      mechanism of, 128
secularism, xxiv
secularization, of Jewish world, 63
   psychoanalysis in answer to, 57
Selbsthass
   Jewish, 80
   of Simone Weil, 62, 82
   self-analysis, Freud's, 126, 129, 142
Semi, A. A., xxviii, xxix, 141–151
Sigmund Freud Center, Hebrew University of Jerusalem, xxix
sin, original, 22–23, 45
Smith, R., 22
socialism, xxiv, 69
   for imbeciles, antisemitism as, 73
   and Jews, 59
socialist ideal, of Bible, 84
Solms, M., 3–9
Sophocles, 127
Spinoza, B., xxviii, 52, 63
Stalin, J., 84
Stätchen, 110, 111
Strachey, J., 3, 4, 5, 6, 15
superego, abandonment by, 91

superstition, xviii

'Take the Money and Run', 112
talion law, 22
Talmud, xvi, xix
Temko, A., 3
Teresa of Avila, Saint, 62
Terracini, L., 62
Third Reich, 92
Thor, 64
thought, 122, 141
   and feeling, 149
   history of, xxvii
   processes, 122, 123
   renunciation of, 149
   space of, 149
transformations, adaptability to, 97
transmigration of souls, 27

Ur-reste, 126
urbanism, 97

Varnhagen, Rahel, 78, 79
Vermorel, H., 86
Vermorel, M., 86
Versagung [renunciation], 123
Viennese group, 60
Viennese Jewish culture, and psychoanalysis, 96
Viennese Psychoanalytical Society, 43
Vom Rath, 88
Vorstellen [representations], 123

war, 74
   destructive power of, 121
   effect of on attitude to death, 18–20
   effects of, 38
Warburg, A., 69

174 INDEX

Warburg Library, 67
Weil, S., 83
   Selbsthass of, 62, 82
Weininger, O., 81, 82, 134
Weizman, H., 88
Weltanschauung, scientific, xviii
Werfel, F., 59
Winter, J. F., 124
witticism, 104, 106
   vs. joke, 103
   organization of, 99
   psychic dynamisms of, 106
   understanding of, 99
Witz, 99, 105, 106, 110, 111
World War I, xxiv, 83, 85, 89, 121
World War II, 73, 83

Wyler, W., 105

Yerushalmi, Y. H., xxv

Zfat mystics, 63
Zionism, xxiv
   Freud's sympathies with, 86, 138
Zionist movement:
   first congress of, 58
   foundation of, 58
Zionist solution, to antisemitism, 84
Zionists, vs. Bundists, 59
Zola, E., 42, 105
   Freud's lectures on, 43
Zweig, A., 51
   –Freud correspondence, 86–87, 89, 92